Also by Chantell Ilbury and Clem Sunter:

The Mind of a Fox: Scenario Planning in Action, 2001,
Human Rousseau and Tafelberg

Socrates & the Fox: A Strategic Dialogue, 2007,
Human & Rousseau and Tafelberg

Chantell Ilbury Clem Sunter

Games FOXES Play

Planning for *Extraordinary* Times

HUMAN & ROUSSEAU TAFELBERG

Published jointly by Human & Rousseau
and Tafelberg, both divisions
of NB Publishers,
40 Heerengracht, Cape Town

Designed by Jürgen Fomm
and typeset in 11.5 on 14 pt Palatino
Diagrams based on original
designs by Daryl Ilbury
Repro by Scan Shop, Cape Town
Printed and bound by Paarl Print,
Oosterland Street, Paarl,
South Africa

First edition, first impression April 2005
Second impression June 2005
Third impression April 2006
Fourth impression February 2007
Fifth impression July 2009

ISBN: 978-0-7981-4509-1

THIS BOOK IS DEDICATED TO

Our families who are our foundation;
Our friends who stand by us in good
and bad times;
Our colleagues who assisted us in producing
the book in such a professional manner;
Zoleka Hlomuka, the foxiest PA in 44 Main;
and
The fox within you – whoever you are,
wherever you are, and whatever you do.

I Can't . . . or Can I?

Four things I'd been better without
Love, curiosity, freckles and doubt.
DOROTHY PARKER

How often do you change your mind? What causes you to change it? Perhaps a newspaper article, except we tend to read newspapers which accord with our views. Maybe an office memorandum, except they are usually as dull as ditch-water and are ignored unless they contain an implied threat. Actually, it is not easy to change somebody's mind with the written word. Occasionally, a book comes along, like *Animal Farm* by George Orwell, that can do the job. But think about conversation. *That* can change your mind, especially if it is with people you trust and respect. Their gestures, intonations and emotions add strength to the content of what they are saying. You respond. There is an interplay in which you are an active participant. As a consequence, your opinions of people and the future can change. Your views on politics and the economy might also be amended, though less frequently and perhaps to a lesser degree. On the other hand, your moral and religious beliefs may never be swayed either by the written or spoken word.

This book is about conversation. Indeed, we introduce a model later on which serves as an agenda for a strategic conversation. Any organisation can use it to change its mindset. 'Change management' is what some people call it, but to get people to manage differently, you have to change their minds first. Attitudinal shift precedes behavioural change. You will also be introduced to some people who never change their mind. They have an idea and that's it. We call them 'hedgehogs'. The majority of Americans love leaders like that – look at the result of the presidential election in 2004. *Time* named the successful candidate as its person of the year. In fact, the 'hedgehog model' underpins much of the management theory taught at Ivy League business schools in the US. There's even a smash hit in business literature suggesting that only hedgehogs convert from good to great leaders.

But don't you smell a rat here? On the one hand, we are deluged with books on change, change, change, and on the other hand, we are told that real champions don't change their minds. So our favourite animal is not a hedgehog, not a rat, but a fox. The rest of the book is about them. 'Foxes' do change their minds – when they realise they are wrong about something or something better exists out there. Against devout hedgehogs like Thatcher, Reagan and George W. Bush stand foxes like Nelson Mandela and F. W. de Klerk. If they hadn't changed their minds, South Africa would never have experienced the miracle that it did. They compromised. By compromising, they won the game.

Thirdly, this book is about games, the games foxes play. Playing games is second nature to all of us. We learn from early childhood how to play games. In fact, life is a game. You're born, you play the game once, then you die. Unless you believe in reincarnation. In which case, depending on how you performed, you come back as an eagle, a rat . . . or a lawyer!

There's been a methodology around for years, at the heart of which lies game playing. It's called scenario planning. Each scenario is a possible outcome to the game. You weigh up the consequences, then you make a move. The military uses this technique. A few businesses do too. But the best example is a country that used scenario planning to improve the quality of its conversation about the future – South Africa. Back to those foxes! They were the transition generation. You can say that South Africans are natural foxes. So are scenario planners. They all have the ability to change their minds; and change other people's minds as well. Where else than in South Africa would you find ex-Marxists and trade unionists becoming chairmen of some of the foremost companies in the land?

I can't . . . or can I? Thank heavens, Dorothy Parker admitted to curiosity and doubt. She was a fox, even though she wanted to be a freckle-less hedgehog.

Anyone for a game?

"'Tis all a Chequer-board of Nights and Days
Where Destiny with Men for Pieces plays:
Hither and thither moves, and mates and slays,
And one by one back in the Closet lays."

RUBÁIYÁT OF OMAR KHAYYÁM

There is a royal and ancient game that for centuries was the enviable pursuit of princes and noblemen, but which has, over the past hundred years, found a home in the heart of the common man (and woman). It demands of the player a passion and precision of movement that can become all-encompassing. The game is, in essence, played as an individual pursuit. However, there is a regular occasion when a team from America finds itself up against the might of Europe, when old hands play shoulder to shoulder with future stars in a genial, yet ruthless, display of mastery of this seemingly genteel game. Each time these teams compete against each other, the battlefield is littered with the stripped confidence of icons and the shattered aspirations of Young Turks; and it is virtually guaranteed that the Americans will lose.

No, it's not the Ryder Cup and golf. It's that other courteous blood sport – chess. Not in the same league you might say when it comes to capturing public attention; but the event we are about to describe made it to the front page of the *Wall Street Journal*. Every year since 1978, member countries of the North Atlantic Treaty Organisation have converged on a venue to compete in the ultimate game of strategy and tactics. Soldiers and civilians, representing some of the finest minds of the Western military establishment, battle it out in what is the only international military chess competition in the world. To some people this may sound a little quaint; but the fact remains that the current world economic, social and political landscape has been shaped by centuries of conflict, often driven by leaders who honed their strategic and tactical abilities playing chess. Napoleon, for example, was a strong player of the game, and Prince Grigori Potemkin, whose conquests expanded the borders of the Russian empire in the eighteenth century, was so addicted to the game that he often commanded junior officers to engage in games of chess in front of him so that he could study the strategies that unfolded.

What is interesting about this annual NATO military chess tournament is that America, which dominates the alliance in most other ways, never seems to do all that well, and Germany invariably emerges the victor. The success of Germany is normally attributed to that country's universal conscription of eighteen-year-old males into its armed forces. Their diverse background provides a wide range of playing strategies. The failure of the American military chess team to win has generally been explained by the relative unpopularity of chess in that country, and the fact that most of its leading players are involved in real combat around the world. However, Germany's dominance in the tournament is about to be challenged by the inclusion of former Warsaw Pact countries into NATO. This move will introduce exciting new teams of players who promise to raise the level of the game, because they grew up under the shadow of the Russian chess superpower next door. Against that, America and Britain's performance will probably improve over time. Why's that? Madonna and Harry Potter have taken up the game and increased its popularity among children.

The Ancient Greek term *strategos* originally denoted a commander-in-chief (or chief magistrate) in Athens. Its meaning then mutated into the art that person was supposed to possess, namely the art of projecting and directing the larger military movements and operations of a campaign. Strategy, as the word is known in English today, is very much part of the vocabulary of military leaders. On one occasion, George W. Bush described his job of Commander-in-Chief of the US Armed Forces as setting the strategic direction in Iraq and ensuring that the generals were given the resources *they* estimated were required for the job. Strategy has also developed into a corporate buzzword used by CEOs.

Strangely though, the chess analogy has not crossed from the war room to the boardroom. Nor has the concept of games generally.

For example, we talk of war games but seldom if ever mention business games – and certainly not business chess. Perhaps the reason for this is that generals know before they go into battle that there are a whole set of conditions over which they have no control and about which they have little knowledge other than what military intelligence has gathered (and we know how reliable that can be!) So they play games and simulate the different paths the battle can take. If the enemy does this, we'll respond in this way, and if the enemy does that, we'll respond with a different tactic. Alternatively, if we initiate a particular battle plan, how will the enemy respond and what are the consequences of each response and how will we counter-respond?

Maybe the cause of the lack of this kind of reasoning (or rather imagination) in the boardroom is that businesses are out to make money, and prefer to do their own thing in meeting this goal. They see themselves as an island in the sea of the market. They aren't overly adversarial to other players unless they have to be, and it is not a matter of life and death. Yes, they may have to take out a few competitors on the way; but it is not the prime purpose of business to defeat the enemy. So, unlike the military, they feel no need to play games to figure out the nature of the competitors' response. CEOs, moreover, feel much more in control in the business world than generals in a war situation because they are not subject to the extremely rude awakenings that war sometimes has to offer. They don't have thousands of unnecessary casualties to contend with if their strategy proves incorrect. They lead relatively pampered lives away from the field of operations. In fact, the nearest they get to a declaration of war is a hostile takeover bid.

The control paradigm in business is further intensified by the linear strategic planning techniques offered by many of the great business schools in America and Europe. The common thread running through these techniques is: select a single set of assumptions; base your plan on those assumptions; then mobilise your troops in support of the plan. Such an approach is actually far removed from the methods now taught at West Point and Sandhurst to cope with today's security threats. On top of that, management consultancies tend to make control and certainty a centrepiece of the particular formula they want to peddle, on the basis that clients pay for precise answers to their problems. They know, like doctors, that their clients don't want 'iffy' advice. Then, overlaying the business schools and consultancies are the 'Billy

Grahams' of business – the immaculately frightful televangelists who twice a year conduct global seminars by satellite and whose stock in trade is oozing confidence about their particular message.

Gurus can't appear doubtful about the future – at least not in public!

The ironic result of all this is that military personnel are much better trained to handle surprises and uncertainty than their business executive counterparts. They are humbler in their expectations but nimbler in their responses. Business whiz kids often think of themselves as smarter than the stuffy breed of person who joins the army, particularly as the former are paid so much more. In reality, many of those kids – particularly the ones who have MBAs – simply don't possess the degree of flexibility (or mental agility) required in war games. The more confident they are, the more linear their approach tends to be in assessing the future. They don't change their minds. Instead, they focus on the short term because that's where their bonuses direct them to look. They forget the old acronym: one battle does not win the war (though it's a heck of a lot better than losing the battle).

Hence the reason for this book – to introduce military-type thinking to business people. Not of the command / control kind, which is the stuff of the thousands of motivational epics which land on the bookshelves each year. No, we're more interested in the games, the scenarios, the risks, the show-stopping discontinuities that are now part and parcel of the world at war as well as the world at peace. Think of the American Marines and the British Special Air Services or the SAS. When they're called in for an assault on an enemy position, they have scale models, they have an understanding of the modus operandi and probable behaviour of the enemy, they visit every scenario over and over again in their game plan. Nevertheless, they know the limits to their knowledge and are ready to adapt spontaneously to any completely unexpected development.

We are qualified to give this alternative picture. In our last book, *The Mind of a Fox*, published in June 2001, we offered a very specific world-view to George W. Bush in the first months of his first term as US president. In an open letter to him, we painted a picture of a world increasingly divided, a world in which the nature of war had changed completely, where terrorist groups could basically build a nuke off the internet; where his prime risk was a massive terrorist strike on a Western city, and where the strategies and tactics to win a war on terror were totally different to those employed in conventional warfare.

We received an interesting comment from an American woman who bought our book at the airport to read on an overnight flight to New York on September 10, 2001. She finished it before she went to sleep, and subsequently recalled that the only thing she thought was ridiculously over the top was our suggestion that terrorism could redefine George Bush's presidency (the word was only mentioned once in the lead-up to the 2000 election). Then she woke up to the announcement that the plane was being diverted because of the terrorist strike. The rest, as they say, is history.

The 9/11 Commission in Washington recently reported that the principal reason for the intelligence agencies failing to detect the plot beforehand was a 'failure of imagination'. We imagined it – albeit using a scenario of nukes being planted in the middle of a city as opposed to planes being flown into tall buildings. We were vaguely right because we never underestimated the sophistication and patience of modern terrorist organisations, combined with a deep resentment and religious hatred of the West. And it's much better being vaguely right than precisely wrong. That's where games are central to envisioning the future. Interestingly,

Rudy Giuliani – the mayor of New York at the time of 9/11 – confirms this approach with his phrase 'relentless preparation'. All the emergency service departments in New York had gone through the drills for a plane crash in the city (one had even been simulated). So even though no one imagined planes being used as missiles to hit buildings, the evacuation and fire drills were similar to a plane crash and saved thousands of lives on the day. In other words, the exact scenario does not have to materialise for the process to pay off.

At this juncture, we feel obliged to point out some significant differences between games and the real world. In a game of chess, for example, the rules never change. Bishops move diagonally, rooks horizontally and vertically, and victory is achieved when the king is checkmated. In life, only the moral rules don't change. All the other rules can and do change and have to be examined before moves can be contemplated. And the meaning of victory in a field like business can differ from person to person. In chess, the gameboard never changes shape and will always have 64 squares, half white, half black. In business, you can change the shape of the gameboard yourself and so can your opponent. The number of squares can grow or shrink; and irrationality, emotion, greed, fear, envy and anger can turn the colours of the squares into every shade of the rainbow. The whole gameboard can even be tipped over temporarily by external events like the bombing in Bali. In chess, the players move the pieces. In the real world, the pieces can take on a life of their own and resist being pushed around if they feel it is not in their best interest – like nonaligned nations and employees.

All in all, business is much more complicated than chess, and demands greater imagination. Business strategy is therefore more of an art than a science (just like war). It is not a game to be played by planners who are solely analysts and believe that the future is a projection of the past. The future is never like the past, because there is always something new, something different. The gift of intuition, the gift of capturing the extraordinary, are therefore vital ingredients in playing successfully on life's gameboard. These are talents that foxes possess – but more of that anon.

Straight talk about strategy

In politics, the path from A to B is never straight.
It almost always goes through C, D or F.

L. PAUL BREMER

During Victorian times, travelling abroad was a real mission. It was not simply a case of weighing anchor and setting sail, it was about planning for a major adventure. So it was a strategic decision to go overseas and choose a foreign destination. Subsequently a series of disciplined tactical manoeuvres had to be executed in order to implement the strategy: what coach to take you from home to the harbour; where to stay before embarkation; which ship to be a passenger on; when best to sail; what provisions to take in addition to the ship's own fare; what medications to pack, etc. (the choice in those days was fairly limited and certainly did not include seasick pills). For the captain of the ship, the operational decisions that needed to be made in order to arrive at the destination were somewhat grander: what provisions to take for the entire complement of crew and passengers, what to do if extreme weather conditions prevailed, at which ports to replenish stocks, what spares to have on board during the voyage, etc.

The sailing metaphor is a useful one to explain the difference between *strategy* and *tactics*. Strategy is about where you are going. Tactics is about how to get there (including logistics). Once you've set off on the voyage, there are only two strategic decisions you can make: change the ultimate destination or cancel the journey altogether and go home. Everything else is tactics. If you stray off course on account of difficult weather, getting back on course is a tactic. If you are becalmed, how to ration the food is a tactic. If you are in danger of being attacked by pirates, steering clear of them is a tactic. Make no mistake, being an expert tactician is as important as being an expert strategist. If you're a bad tactician, you can sail the boat into the rocks and lose all life and goods on board. But they are different functions.

An old nineteenth-century saying sums it up quite well: "Strategy differs materially from tactic; the latter belonging only to the mechanical movement of bodies, set in motion by the former." In other words, a handful of strategic decisions determine all future operational decisions. Yet so many businesses confuse strategy with tactics. They spend three days having a strategic workshop of which a couple of hours are spent on strategy and the rest of the time on operational matters which are totally subsidiary to strategy. We have found that in the largest of companies a genuine strategic conversation covering *all* the bases and unearthing the deepest issues need take no longer than four to five hours, on average a day or, comfortably stretching it, two days. The topic is after all about the commanding heights of the business and there the landscape is relatively simple, with only a few issues needing resolution.

Understandably, it makes sense to have this type of strategic conversation before the start of the normal annual planning cycle, the purpose of which is to put together next year's production targets and budget. The latter constitute the steps on the road to the company's long-term destiny, so it is prudent to have a discussion about where the road leads beforehand. Nevertheless, as you will see later on, we do make accommodation in our strategic conversation model for some discourse on tactics. This acts as a warm-up for the operational planning meetings and sets some broad parameters for them. In addition, we want to ensure that the strategy session doesn't end up in a haze of hot air where nobody is going to pick up on anything afterwards. So many strategy workshops are instantly forgotten as soon as people return to the office. They remember the parties in the evening and the chat in the pub, but nothing more.

In conversations around strategy, one could say that the best strategists are the marksmen of the boardroom – the archers who put their fingers to the wind before drawing back their bow (absorbing the context before letting the arrow fly). They understand the meaning of the catch phrase 'ready . . . aim . . . fire'. 'Aim' is strategy and 'fire' the tactics. It sounds logical, but it is often implemented the other way around. Many businesses, especially those run by brash young entrepreneurs, indulge in 'ready . . . fire . . . aim'. That is, they rush into action and then dream up the rationalisation afterwards. It's okay if by some fluke you hit the target, but wild misses are the normal result. A case of hubris, then nemesis. Apologies all round. Reload. And the worst thing is implementing a winning tactic in the short run, only to find that it triggers a response which is totally unanticipated and ruins your strategy in the long run. It's called the law of unintended consequences.

On the opposite side of the fence, other businesses, especially those with a penchant for an excessively bureaucratic or participative style of management, end up in an everlasting cycle of "ready . . . aim . . . have a workshop . . . aim . . . have a conference . . . aim . . . have a summit . . . aim . . . and if all else fails, bring in the consultants and establish a subcommittee of the board . . . aim . . ." They never fire because they never establish a target to aim at. They don't change their minds. They never make their minds up!

These last two approaches to strategy are obviously wrong. The right approach can be summed up in the following diagram, which hopefully hits home:

Chart 1 ***The Shooting Range***

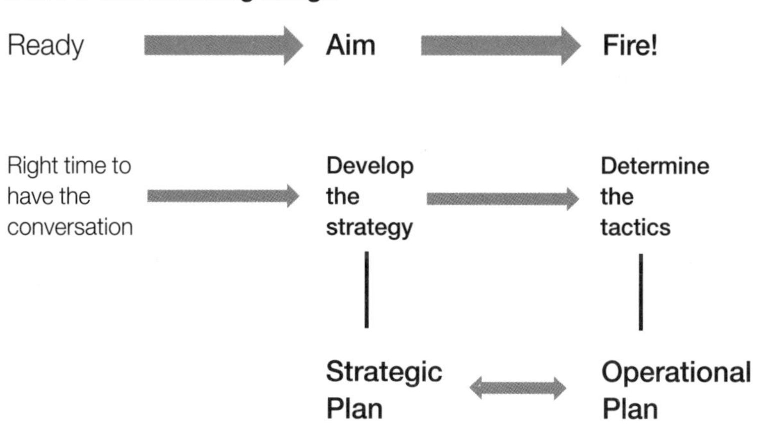

However, there is one thing that's incorrect about this diagram, which is very difficult to represent on paper. When looking at the future, you're always shooting at a moving target. The dynamics can change just like that. So ahead of pulling the trigger or releasing the bowstring, it is essential to play the game of *what if*. Not to be paralysed into inaction, we stress, but to adapt if necessary and maybe take one or two of the *what ifs* out of play with a pre-emptive strategy. Seasoned sea captains – or sea dogs as they were called in Elizabethan times – recognised the benefit of this method by considering the following kinds of questions before embarking on an ocean voyage:

- What if one of our ports of call falls into the hands of our enemies?

- What if key members of the crew fall ill or die?
- What if unfavourable weather conditions play havoc with our schedule?
- What if conditions at our final destination are too hostile?

Notice that the *what ifs* were all relevant. They weren't vague anxieties inviting the retort 'so what?' The captains didn't necessarily have the answers before they set sail. But they were mentally prepared for surprises. It was part of the 'ready' phase to consider possibilities of having to readjust the 'aim' (strategy) or 'fire' (tactics) in the event of unfortunate scenarios.

Alas, many forms of strategic thinking popular today assume that the future can be represented by a fixed straight line. It's a sign of the control we think we have over the environment. One such model can be depicted like this:

Context → ends → means → resources → implementation and control. No crooked thoughts in here! No options.

Now just play the scenario of going into a restaurant and asking for a menu. The waiter brings it over but it only has one item on it. You complain there's no choice. He retorts: "Ah, but the chef guarantees that the dish is better cooked this year than last year." You would not be satisfied. Yet this is precisely how companies using a linear model discuss the future. How can we do the *same thing* better?

We prefer to think of the future as a cone of uncertainty that opens up over time – the further away from the present moment you are, the greater the degree of uncertainty.

In terms of planning, therefore, a short-term strategy of say six months to a year is quite easy to develop with a budget and a set of measurable outcomes in place to monitor progress. The decisions are in fact more tactical than strategic, more about the practical means of getting there than the end in itself.

Chart 2 ***The Cone of Uncertainty I***

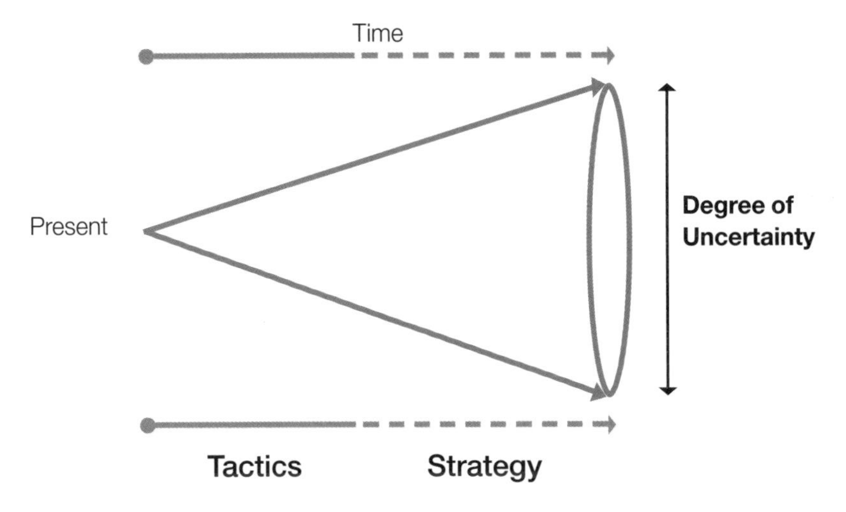

By contrast, as the cone of uncertainty expands over time, long-term strategy demands more flexibility and imagination. You may even have to question the purpose of the mission, as well as the means of accomplishing it. This is clear for two reasons: the further away the future is from the present, the greater the degree of uncertainty it entails; and the more numerous are the factors beyond your control. This explains why many CEOs would rather be measured on the success of their short-term tactics than their long-term strategies. They want to make sure of next year's bonus in case they have to bow out. Such a corporate planning environment does not encourage the long-term viability of companies. As each CEO goes through the revolving door and the new one is ushered in, the strategy changes. This has spawned a whole new field of 'change management' techniques served up as instant remedies to organisations perpetually in a crisis mode. Yet the crisis originated in short-term strategies wholly at odds with each other, and wholly at odds with creating sustainable growth in the long run.

Generally, businesses operating within more developed markets should find it easier to change strategic direction because they employ more sophisticated planning techniques and have the resources to do so. Furthermore, it could be argued that in these more developed markets there is less uncertainty, because the conditions are more established than those in developing countries where the challenges are greater and strategic decisions taken by businesses are therefore more courageous. But it actually turns out to be the other way round. CEOs in the West completely misread the tea leaves in the arrogant belief that they can shape the future their way, whereas their Third World colleagues interpret the patterns before drinking the tea. The cup is their 'cone of uncertainty'.

Amazing, too, are the number of Western books on leadership which focus solely on charisma and inspiration. Leadership is also about picking the right strategy. There's no point in marching your troops over the hill, however inspired they may be, if it's the wrong hill. So if as a leader you don't have a strong sense of direction, choose a strategist (or scout) who has. On the one hand, he may save you from abominable decisions which lead you down the precipitate path to failure. On the other hand, he may discover the best way to the top in the most unlikely of circumstances.

It may be true that improved technological know-how and access to information make it easier for modern businesses to temper external forces and to ride out inclement economic conditions. Yet, the move from an industrial to a knowledge economy, together with globalisation, has seen a huge increase in complexity. Markets are more restless, businesses are more decentralised, decision-making is more diffuse. As businesses widen their influence on the environment, so they are able to influence the environment of the other players in their vicinity. Hence the perception that a company is a self-sufficient island cut off from its competitors is erroneous. Actually, a new form of uncertainty brought about by the interconnected nature of business is emerging, where remote causes way outside of our control and springing from an unknown place on the other side of the world can have major consequences for strategy. Damage control means including those two words: *what if?* They are essential to get a feel for the interconnected complexities that impact on strategy and its execution – in other words, the curved balls the enemy or the environment can throw at you to really mess things up. Imagination, uncertainty, painting relevant scenarios and juggling with options should therefore become second nature to us. We need to understand the full measure of choice, as it underpins our decision-making process.

So, we're asking you to break out of your traditional planning habits. And, if you *are* willing to be a bit of a rebel, the secret to dealing with the future and planning for extraordinary times lies in conversation.

The power of the spoken word

Speak to me pretty, speak to me nice;
Quote me those wonderful phrases, once or twice.
BRENDA LEE

The true nature of communication lies not in the grammatical structure and content of the text but in its intended (sender) and interpreted (receiver) meaning. In conversations, it is sometimes something that is not said that says it all. Emotions and opinions can just as easily be transmitted through bodily behaviour: a shrug of the shoulders, a nod of the head, a smile or a frown. Nonetheless, an emotionally laden conversation that is not properly managed can leave unresolved issues that will threaten the stability of any agreement and the sustainability of any relationship. In a strategic conversation, such unresolved issues could undermine the integrity of the entire process and derail it. Hence, the secret to managing such a conversation lies in the careful examination of its context and the social dynamics between the people having it. This can only be achieved once each participant in the conversation has an idea of the possible sources of ignorance and misunderstanding that could filter out the true meaning of elements in the conversation. In business, particularly, any conversation around strategy runs the risk of not achieving its desired outcome if a clear picture of the interests of the participants and the business model they're using is not achieved. Not only does this hinder alignment, but it also leaves strategic value on the table.

So, how is it possible to interpret the course of a conversation correctly and harness its collective value? The secret is to look beyond what is said and examine what drives it. To understand a conversation's peculiarity – its uniqueness of interplay – it is necessary to be aware of the possible sum of the exchanges in the minds of each person around a table. Recording and minuting are not enough. You have to regard conversation not as a series of simple expression of thoughts, but as an intricate series of games. This not only recognises the 'human-ness' of conversation and places what is expressed in the correct context, but also facilitates the management of the conversation.

There are two byways into the mind: through conversation (involving active listening) and through reading. In any organisation, communication is via both. Whether it is face-to-face, via teleconference, fax, phone or e-mail, we conduct business through the exchanging of information in written, verbal or nonverbal form. The outcome of such communication is determined through the absorption of the content and interpretation of meaning. Because of the very nature of speaking with people as opposed to reading, say, what they have written, conversation provides better insight. The mind is in a more intuitive state, there's minimal emphasis on paper, and the views presented are more spontaneous and based on honest experience. Consequently, for an organisation to cope with choice and to achieve more effective decision-making, strategy must be dealt with through conversation. This is a whole lot better than the circulation of long, monotonous documents with appendices containing computer projections lending dubious authenticity to the exercise.

Depending on the spoken word is nothing new. Before formal currencies were established, business transactions took the form of bartering – two goats were worth one sheep, three sheep were worth one cow, and three cows could be exchanged for one wife plus, if you were good at bartering, a keg of ale. Although today currency puts a price on commodities, people still put a value on price. For this reason most business transactions, except those that take place in countries ruled by ruthless dictators, still involve an open exchange of conversation between buyer and seller.

In the third millennium, things haven't changed all that much. Every day, in our social life and in business, we conduct conversations that fill the 'space' between us. The purpose of conversations is essentially twofold – to establish, maintain and develop social bonds; and to communicate ideas with the intention of attaining an outcome. Whereas the first form of conversation is *social*, the latter is *strategic*. Of course there are occasions when the two forms of conversation overlap, such as in the mind of a young man chatting up a girl on a first dinner date! Because there is an intended outcome in a strategic conversation, whether it is to secure the last slice of apple pie at a hungry family reunion, or to finalise the merger of two multinationals, the success of the outcome is determined by how the conversation is managed.

Continuing the example of the young man on a first date, the outcome of the carefully managed conversation will be measured afterwards in distance from each other on the couch.

Surely a desired outcome that is achieved without a properly managed conversation is still the desired outcome? Maybe so, in the short term. But the long term is about relationships and trust based on handshakes, not lawyers. It makes sense that only a strategic conversation that is properly mastered will lay a secure foundation for such bonds to be forged. How many negotiations have failed because badly managed conversations left value on the table? How many managers have been toppled because they left in their path a wake of conversational debt?

So is such a strategic conversation possible? Yes, if the very factors that challenge strategy over time – increased uncertainty and reduced control – are an integral part of the conversation. This was the essence of the prototype model which we introduced in *The Mind of the Fox*. We wanted executives to confront the unknown, to accept that we haven't scraped the surface of the top molecule on the very tip of the iceberg in understanding the world around us. We wanted them to begin the conversation blessed with that essential quality possessed by all true explorers – humility. Not for one minute were we suggesting that they should dive hell for leather into the void offered up by the future. Leaping off a proverbial bridge will only reward a business executive with a new perspective in life if he has a bungee cord tied to his ankles first. Otherwise, he is dead meat.

So what is this bungee cord made of? We venture wisdom. The use of this term is often accompanied by images of a skinny old man in a loincloth with a long silvery-grey beard. He is perched on the steps of a monastery clinging to the slopes of a mountain. Actually, you don't have to be old or know a lot to be wise. The essence of wisdom lies not so much in knowledge per se, but rather in the manner in which knowledge is put to use. More importantly, wisdom demands a certain scepticism about all claims of knowledge, because more is unknown and uncertain than known and certain. The result is a ceaseless flow of movement between confidence and doubt; and it is this fine line between them that a wise person walks, using logic when he is confident and imagination when he is in the dark.

Chart 3 ***The Prototype Matrix***

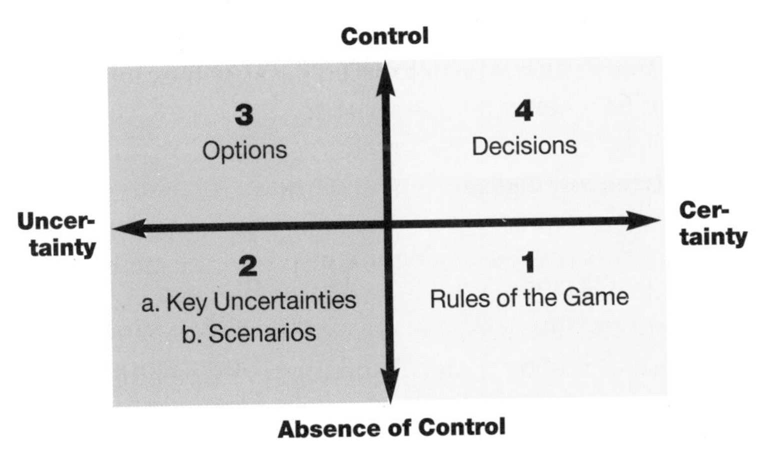

So we came up with a simple matrix that compelled top management to ask two questions in discussing the future of their business and designing their strategies:

1. What do you and do you not control?
2. What is certain and uncertain about the future?

We started in the bottom right-hand quadrant by asking them to consider the factors beyond their control but certain to govern their lives. We then tested their imagination on key uncertainties which might affect the progress of the company and what scenarios might ensue. We then moved to the control side and stimulated a wide-ranging discussion of options to meet the challenges posed by the scenarios, before asking them to put a stake in the ground on decisions. It worked. Sales of *The Mind of a Fox* exceeded 50 000 and many companies from leading multinationals to small and medium-sized businesses in South Africa are now using our technique. Like all models, though, we've been updating the matrix ever since we introduced it. The purpose of *Games Foxes Play* is to set the model out in its present form (it is no longer a matrix, as you will see). Before proceeding to describe the latest version, however, we would like to list three likes and dislikes which have driven us to make the adaptations that we have.

Chart 4 ***Likes and Dislikes***

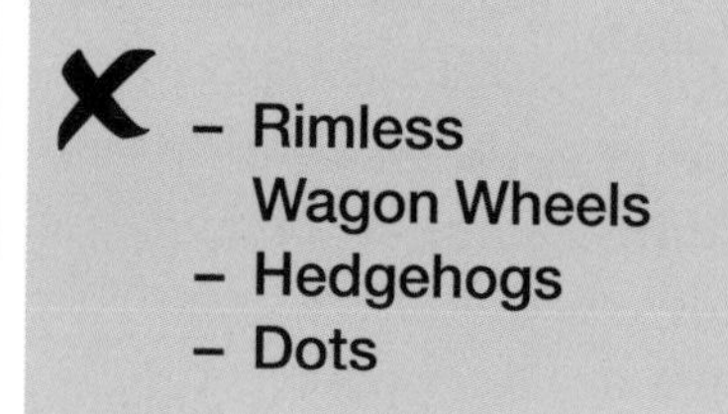

Rimless wagon wheels versus circles

Conversation is a game of circles.
RALPH WALDO EMERSON

Strategic workshops can be frustrating, especially if they are run according to the rimless wagon-wheel approach. At the centre of the accompanying figure is a hub representing the CEO plus his or her close confidantes. They represent the cabal. Emanating out of the hub are the spokes, at the ends

Chart 5 ***Rimless Wagon Wheels***

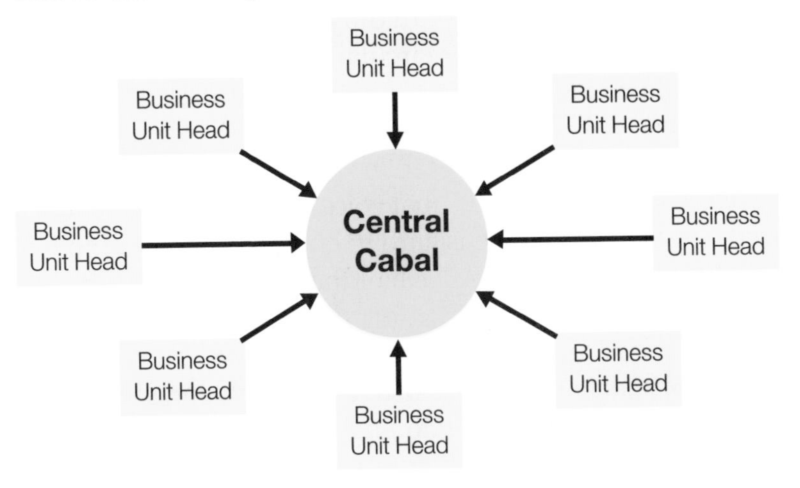

of which are the business units. The sole purpose of the workshop is for the business unit heads to feed their five-year plans and projections into the central cabal, which acts like a gigantic sponge absorbing this information. The cabal then decides on overall company strategy in a completely separate forum. The business unit heads never get to participate in such a discussion. They merely talk about their own unit's future. No rim joins them around the periphery because no general conversation takes place on the overall business. They are effectively 'siloed'.

How far west do you think the pioneers of American frontier life would have got if their wagon wheels had been without rims? They would have got bogged down just outside of Boston. But how many companies adopt this approach because of an autocratic CEO who wants to keep strategy all to himself, or maybe include one or two of his close chums? Plenty!

In contrast, we believe in circles when it comes to effective strategic sessions: conversation circles. For the whole business. We believe that the forward movement of a company into extraordinary times can only be ensured if the direction of the conversation is circular. Each part of the conversation tips into the next part in a fairly seamless manner. So in sessions we facilitate we prefer to have the executive team sitting literally at a round table, with everybody in sight of each other and having an equal voice. Sometimes this requires a cultural change which is hard to imagine. In one company, the CEO was nicknamed 'the handbrake' for the dampening effect he had on the conversation. But if it happens the way it should, the results can be truly remarkable. We've had directors privately coming up to us afterwards and saying that it was the best strategy session they had ever attended.

There are reasons. As business organisations grow, they need to draw more and more on the expertise of those within the organisation. Where better to find it than in your top executive team? In the so-called knowledge economy, 'flatter' structures are the embodiment of the modern organisation. They encourage the free flow of ideas and energy between all the elements of the organisation, thereby promoting buy-in and innovation across the board. While some, mainly larger, organisations still cling on to the old hierarchical ladders, most organisations that value creativity encourage ideas to bubble up from below. Approachability is a key characteristic of managers in these new structures. Gone are the days when decisions either 'trickled down' or were 'thrust down', depending on the personality of the heavyweight at the top.

The direction of conversation in a 'flat' structure is more circular. Ideas are passed on for continual assessment, review and adaptation, and subsequently these ideas build momentum and direction. Unlike the spokes of a rimless wagon wheel, the flow of conversation around a circle is, by its very nature, inclusive, and the points are contextualised.

Contributors to the conversation see the value of their input being recognised by peers and more senior and junior staff. More importantly, they are given an opportunity to gain insight and perspective into the reason for the organisation's existence. As scenario strategists, we see the value in extending scenario sage Peter Schwartz's belief that "scenario planning must be intensely participative or it fails". We believe that all planning must be intensely participative or it fails. Hence every level of an organisation should have conversation circles in which strategy is discussed.

Chart 6
Conversation Circles

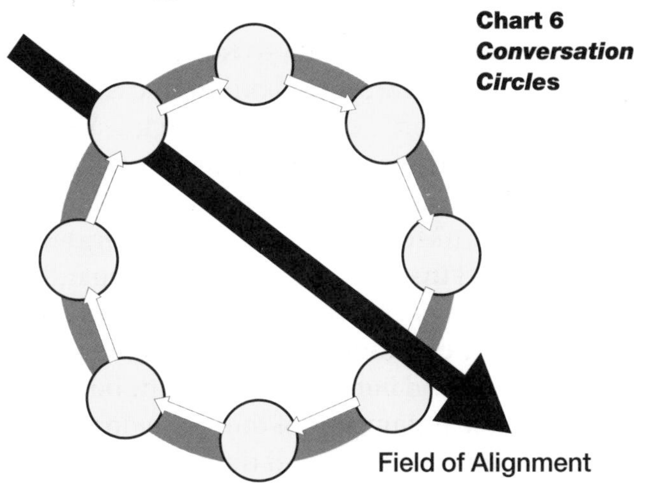

When the strategic conversation is circular, it flows like a current through the heads of all the people sitting around the table, creating its own 'field of alignment'. This method of conversation allows those involved to escape (at least temporarily) from the silos of their business units to capture the bigger picture. They consequently have a better idea of their role in ensuring the company's overall success. A conversation circle has other associated advantages: it encourages a richness that can only come out of diversity, enabling greater insight into the views of people from disparate backgrounds;

it sends a clear message of an organisation's commitment to participative management; and the inclusivity of the process recognises individual input, thereby developing an environment that respects and retains talent. Above all, it's meant to be fun. Not like those sombre affairs where pearls of wisdom are passed down by important people speaking in slow and measured tones to a gathering of staff in the canteen. This is cut and thrust, a chance in a lifetime to air your views. And guess what? People are more creative when they are having fun and feeling relaxed. Think of the atmosphere in the local pub!

For all the reasons given so far, any strategic conversation within an organisation ought to cascade through the entire organisation. Conversation circles should start at the top and work their way down over a period of months. Obviously, the further down you go in the organisation, the more specific the conversation becomes and the more it revolves around the tactical roles departments should play in winning the game. Nevertheless, while the direction of the company may be formulated at the senior executive level, it is important for all employees to understand the company's direction and be part of the strategic thinking process, as this creates alignment and a sense of purpose within the company. Hence, some of the material discussed at CEO level should find its way down, and original comments on it from employees should find their way up. Wisdom is not the preserve of the senior management team alone.

Our recommendation is, in a way, a top-down democratic approach. Not in the narrow sense of democracy which means giving everyone the vote. But in the wider sense of granting people the right to have their say and deliberate on the issues of the moment – business by discussion if you please. If it doesn't happen (and we're afraid that in most companies it doesn't), the employees just come to work to collect their cheques. They're not involved. They don't understand the objectives.Think of two professional soccer teams being requested to play a soccer game for ninety minutes where there are no goalposts. They run around, dribbling here, dribbling there, passing the ball back and forth all over the pitch, then change ends and do exactly the same. There's no score at the end because there are no goals to shoot at. Imagine what that does for the motivation of the two teams and their performance. A variation is to demand that the two teams play the game where there are goalposts but they are being continually shifted. This doesn't do much good for morale either. Yet some CEOs just can't make up their mind on strategy. They chop and change, depending upon which management consultant they have in tow.

As facilitators we don't like prepared papers on strategy. They straitjacket people, put them in a groove. Instead we encourage those involved in our conversation circle just to bring their accumulated knowledge and experience to the table so that they contribute spontaneously to the discussion. We are more concerned with the depth and breadth of the conversation than its length (although as we've mentioned our conversations tend to be much shorter than the average workshop). Primarily we want people to think out of the box.

But let's be frank – inclusive conversation can be a beast to manage and it invariably requires a certain level of harmony and a special kind of leader. Opponents of 'flat' organisational structures, for example, will talk about the dangers of completely open, unstructured conversations that may dilute the decision-making responsibilities of management and slow down the implementation of strategy. This argument is more frequently advanced as a company grows and an established decision structure is essential. The desire for management to control operations in order to ensure the maintenance of focus is understandable; but images of a babbling free-for-all put forward by the more power-retentive management types misconstrue the idea of an 'inclusive conversation'. It is quite possible for strategic conversations to be open and inclusive, but at the same time businesslike and intense – as long as they are carefully structured. Moreover, conversation circles need not interfere with standard lines of authority and decision-making chains, if – like any other function – they are given a specific remit, and are properly scheduled. However, if these words don't alleviate your anxieties, just use our conversation model at the most senior executive level. It will definitely shorten the annual strategy session and make it productive.

Returning to our concept that conversation circles can create a 'field of alignment', they are an ideal tool for resolving conflict between contending parties, each with their own interests and perception of the game. Before negotiations begin in earnest, a strategic conversation along the lines suggested lays the groundwork for a common understanding of the game in which the parties are represented (as well as a mutual understanding of each other's roles). Negotiations have a better chance of success, particularly if the consequences of failure are mapped out in a credible scenario. In this vein, an interesting use of our technique was to structure a discussion on the future of the game bird population in South Africa. Present were the shooters, the environmentalists, the farmers and the safari operators. By the end of the session, everyone was aware of the rules of the game for conserving the unparalleled number of species of game birds that exist in South Africa. Probably the industry in South Africa in most need of such a discussion is the health care industry. What is the role of the public and private sectors in winning the health care game for the country as a whole? What is the downside of losing the game?

Foxes versus hedgehogs

> *You spotted snakes with double tongue,*
> *Thorny hedgehogs, be not seen.*
> WILLIAM SHAKESPEARE

We don't want to repeat all that we said in *The Mind of a Fox* about hedgehogs and foxes. Suffice it to say that we like foxes and dislike hedgehogs (the *human* version that is). The comparison was first introduced by an Ancient Greek poet called Archilochus around 650 B.C. In a fragment of his verse, which has survived to the present day, he said: "The fox knows many things – the hedgehog one big one." Why he chose those two animals to illustrate this difference in thinking we shall never know, because he's been dead for over two and a half millennia. However, his analogy was taken up in the middle of the last century by an eminent British philosopher, Isaiah Berlin, in his famous essay, *The Hedgehog and the Fox*. He wanted primarily to draw a distinction between those philosophers who based their theory on a single idea and, if that idea proved false, the whole theory crumbled; and those philosophers who built up their theory on a variety of observations, and even if several of those observations proved incorrect, the theory could still stand.

Widening Berlin's interpretation to mankind in general, the image of what hedgehogs see ahead of them is narrowed to a central vision. They simplify life around one great idea, more or less disregarding everything else, and bet on that idea. The rewards, if their single idea or theory is correct, are substantial, but then again so is the degree of damage if they are wrong – arguably risky stuff in today's complex, interconnected, uncertain and volatile world. Foxes, on the other hand, know many things, and regard life as a balancing act between competing claims. Foxes think of life as a system composed of many parts and interdependencies, and it is only through the knowledge of the system as a whole that one can optimise decisions about the future. A critical difference between human hedgehogs and foxes is that the former like to think they are in control whereas the latter know they are never fully in control. The success of foxes therefore lies in their adaptability to their external environment and the resourcefulness of their responses. Followers of foxes and hedgehogs will notice the difference in trails they leave behind. Fox prints weave to and fro through forests, avoiding dangerous spots and approaching possible sources of nutritional value. Hedgehog steps never deviate from the chosen path. This is why members of the Hedgehog Preservation Society in the UK build small tunnels underneath the motorways, so that they can cross unhurt.

Nonetheless, there are plenty of admirers of hedgehogs around. Jim Collins, in his bestseller *Good to Great*, argues that companies that embrace a hedgehog philosophy and are focused on a single path are more likely to succeed in what they set out to do. He goes on: "For a hedgehog, anything that does not somehow relate to the hedgehog idea holds no relevance." We contend that employing such a high-risk strategy is increasingly incongruent with the interdependent world we live in, and can steer dangerously close to fanaticism. Fundamentalists are by definition hedgehogs. Nevertheless, we don't have any problem with focus, particularly when it means the opposite of scatterbrained. Foxes *are* focused, but also possess whiskers to pick up the sensitivities and interests of the players around them. And they are just as prepared to stand on *moral* principles as hedgehogs, but not on ideas and dogma.

In the business world hedgehogs seek an *optimal* strategy (for everlasting growth), whereas foxes are after a robust strategy which will see them through the bad times in order to prosper in the good times. Nothing more, nothing less. We prefer the fox's humbler but less brittle approach, because it gives you a better chance of being around in the longer run. As Albert Einstein is reputed to have said: "You can simplify things as much as possible, but don't make them simpler than they should be."

Dots in space versus games

The military makes a great hammer,
but not every problem is a nail.

GENERAL HUGH SHELTON
Former Chairman of the US Joint Chiefs of Staff

You may be forgiven for thinking that strategic planning sometimes drives you dotty. Dots are what companies come out with at the end of strategy sessions. Dot: "We are going to double our production in five years." Dot: "We are going to grow our bottom line at 10 per cent per annum in real terms." So what's the problem? Organisations have used this method for decades. You set a goal and head off; after all, organisations need direction.

The problem comes when the dot is set in space. The CEO issues a strategic directive and everybody falls into line without knowing or questioning the context of the dot. It becomes mesmerising. Anything said about it is without nuance or qualification. It hypnotises people into doing imprudent, irresponsible and sometimes downright dishonest things to achieve the dot. Moreover, when the environment changes, everybody still clings to the dot. Even when the dot has gone spectacularly beyond its sell-by date, the troops still march on (particularly if someone was stupid enough to publish the dot in the first place). We've all had these dots on our horizons at some time in our lives and been fixated by them. Some are harmless, some dangerous. Some are even terminal, such as when you continue to watch the dot as you fall off the cliff. By now you will have guessed: dots in space are the single ideas beloved by hedgehogs. They convert uncertainties into facts to keep the dot alive and, worse still, twist the facts altogether when pressure really mounts. For a big enough dot, hedgehogs are not above 'sexing up' intelligence dossiers by hardening the language here and there.

Nonetheless, we don't dislike dots as long as they are put in context. Indeed, you will see in our model that dots are the equivalent of the measurable outcomes we insist are part of the conversation before it is wrapped up. But before agreeing on dots, you must understand the context in which they are made, so that, should the context change, the dots can be revised.

In the last section, we asserted that foxes were systems thinkers. But we don't like the word 'system' for two reasons. It is too abstract a word to describe business, which after all is a flesh-and-blood affair run by human beings for human beings. It implies that if you have enough information about the system, the outcome may be predicted, whereas business is inherently unpredictable, precisely because human beings are unpredictable. We prefer the word 'game', because games *are* played by human beings and can have unpredictable results. Hence the rest of this book is about games.

Edward Arlington Robinson once said: "Life is a game that must be played." The reality is that life is a series of *sub-games*. A sub-game in this context is any form of interaction between two or more people – let's call them *players* – where the intention of each player is to achieve some measure of gain for themselves. The word 'gain' should be interpreted here in the widest possible sense of being spiritual or material, short term or long term. Every sub-game has its own set of rules, scoring system, rewards and punishments; and features people who are on your side in the game, against you, or are ambivalent – in other words neutral.

A sub-game can also involve any interaction between a person and his or her environment. So, whether we like it or not, from the moment we scream our first breath to when we sigh our last we are locked in a series of adventures with people and the environment around us, with the aim of securing that certain degree of gain. Like players on a field, whether we are crying for a feed, trying to cheat death or simply surviving a trying day, we strategise to win over our adversaries and adversities, physical and otherwise. In short – we *play* games all our lives, either as individuals or in teams.

Some people might dismiss the concept of life being a game – or more realistically a series of sub-games – as flippant. Nothing could be further from the truth. Sub-games can be highly complex and are both sequential and concurrent in their timing and location. An example of sequential sub-games would be the emotional, intellectual and social games employed during the educational path from preprimary school to employment. Primary schooling is normally spent in sub-games, where the dynamics are underpinned by the developing of the child's curiosity and the entrenching of the school's authority. Secondary schooling and the growth of individual self-confidence support an environment that encourages sub-games of negotiation. College or university sparks sub-games of rebellion that are then reined in when the reality of a pay cheque requires playing in the more structured sub-games of business.

More challenging is the balancing of concurrent sub-games, like those between business and family. Working harder may bring in more money but it may be at the expense of valuable family time. Concurrent games call for decisions around trade-offs that in turn may have long-term consequences. An example would be a busy parent's cancelling of an important business trip to attend a school sports day or school play. The parent may not remember but the child certainly will (even more so if you don't pitch up).

Because humans are social animals, most of the games we play are naturally with other humans and are conducted through the medium of *conversation* and *behaviour*. Conversation in this sense is the exchanging of verbal and written information, whereas behaviour is nonverbal and non-written and often differs in intent and content. These two functions apply as much on a school playground as they do in the boardrooms of giant multinationals.

The secret to the difference between merely having a conversation, or acting out a role in any game, and securing genuine and permanent gains, is the employment of effective strategies which rely on *knowing how to play the game*. This presumes among other things: understanding the game; respecting the fact that there are interdependencies between all the players with each having expectations about the other's behaviour; and a flexible attitude which acknowledges that games are risky and sometimes demand radical shifts in strategy. The best course of action therefore necessitates the successful consolidation of the information at your disposal at any one time into a level of knowledge and wisdom which allows you a fair chance of winning the game. This book is designed to give you the tools to do just that.

Effective strategy not only involves knowing *how* to play the game, but also knowing *what* game to play. Put yourself in the position of a student about to select a career. Now picture careers as games, each with its own rules. Now match your strengths and weaknesses to each game and ask which game suits you best. How many students go through that process? How many career officers understand the rules of each career game when advising their young clients? This is the time in your life when you are at your most free to choose, because once the career is chosen, you are subject to its rules. Moreover, entry into any game comes with a cost. There is the direct cost of obtaining the qualifications to enter that game. Think how much it costs to become a doctor or engineer. Then there is the opportunity cost of all the other careers you are passing up in order to pursue your selected option. If you choose, you refuse. Fast forward to being an adult and try the negotiation game. It is clearly one of give and take. If you are going to play, you have to be prepared to *give*. Marriages that last are all about that.

Equally, effective strategy means knowing when a game has *changed* to the point that you either have to adapt to the new rules, or plan an exit. As we've already mentioned, the difference between real life and chess is that in real life the rules can change, whereas in chess the rules define the game and are therefore set in concrete. For example, the rules of a particular business sector can be changed so much by advances in technology that it is no longer recognisable as the sub-game it was. Winners become losers and new winners emerge. Look at how much radio has been changed by TV!

Some of our readers might say at this stage that theories on games and how to play them already exist. We will touch on all of them. However, what sets this book apart is its presentation of a new approach – which we have dubbed *The Conversation Model* – that combines elements of Game Theory, Chaos Theory and Systems Thinking. Crucially, we have ensured that our model is understandable by ordinary people making everyday decisions. It is plain common sense. One of the problems of the aforementioned theories is that they are mathematically so advanced that only a fraction of decision-makers use them, even though they contain valid and extremely relevant material for today's competitive and uncertain world. They also ignore the passions, emotions and arbitrariness of real-life human beings playing real-life games. David Hume, the eighteenth-century Scottish philosopher, was spot on with his take on human nature: reason is the slave of passion, he said, not the other way around. Even in the age of electronics and information technology, we are still messy, unpredictable entities. Thus, we have taken the best ingredients of each of the above theories and, with the addition of Scenario Planning, come up with a method as close to real life as possible. And it is very popular because everybody understands the concept of a game from early infancy.

How can we be so sure? Simply, the overwhelming response we have had from the diverse array of individuals and businesses who have used our material to improve their handling of the future and the way they implement decisions. Whether the group comprises bankers, miners, bishops, broadcasters, doctors, scientists, teachers or lawyers (not recycled) – they love playing games. They are seduced into lowering their guard because games are, well, something to enjoy. They take the sting out of reality.

As you will soon see, we have also developed over the last three years a set of visual aids to assist the conversation about every aspect of the game. Specifically in business, we have discovered that the visual medium is the best way to surface the instincts and intuition of the top executive team and get them to air their views in a creative, but structured manner. Practical people don't like dealing in purely abstract concepts. They like visual stimuli, since the eye is directly wired to the imagination. Moreover, numbers, though vital in the end for budgets and operational plans, bog down discussions on subjects like risks, uncertainties and scenarios because so much of what is important about the future cannot be quantified with any precision. The issues have to be handled in a more open forum. Hence, we prefer to play a series of mind games with our clients, which may lead them in directions they never expected to go. But the result is a comprehensive picture of the gameboard they're playing on as well as the tactics available in different positions on the board.

We see our job in this book as encouraging decision-makers to re-perceive the future in such a way that they are not often caught off guard (never say never!). They know the game they are in and how to play the game, whatever surprises are thrown at them. We want to persuade people to put on the equivalent of night-vision goggles so that threats (as well as opportunities) are more clearly visible than the naked eye will allow. We want to train the mind to penetrate the opaqueness that inevitably envelops the future – to see emerging shapes as it were – in a real and practical manner. We want people to recognise the fact that games are filled with controllables and non-controllables, certainties and non-certainties, and that true competitive advantage lies in accepting the paradox.

The opinion that life is a series of games has, by obvious association, the assumption that as players we strive to win over others. It is, whether we like it or not, in our nature. The respected evolutionary biologist, Professor Richard Dawkins, suggests in *The Selfish Gene* that our need to win against others and protect our self-interest is in our genes. We are all simply survival machines built by a short-lived confederation of long-lived genes that have replicated and adapted over time to changing conditions, threats and opportunities. Genes are the primary policy-maker; brains are the executive. However, as our brains have become more highly developed, they have taken over more and more of the actual policy decisions, using tricks like learning and simulation to do so. Thus games – and the enjoyment of winning them – are central to our development of strategies for survival.

Anyone who follows sport has experienced the agony and ecstasy of losing and winning. That's the essence of the game.

If games were predictable they wouldn't be fraught with the emotion surrounding the uncertainty of their outcome. We would be prepared for every eventuality; the fun would go out of sport; and there would be no such thing as bookies, ups, downs, celebrations and commiserations – which sound more like our lot in life.

Given our definition of the word 'game', and in terms of the number of players, it could be argued that, other than staying alive, the most *popular* game played in the world is the game of *business*. Think about it: every single day of the year billions of people all over the world strategise in social, economic, emotional and intellectual games with each other in the hope of achieving some measure of gain such as a momentary nod of approval from a superior; influencing a departmental discussion; closing a deal; securing cash in the bank; robbing competitors of market share; or getting the upper hand in some corporate power struggle. Every day some people win and some people lose. We are going to help you to win.

The Conversation Model

Being President is like running a cemetery. You've got a lot of people under you, but nobody's listening.
BILL CLINTON

Some people get things wrong, some famously so. For all his faults, Bill Clinton was a great listener, even if he felt his subordinates weren't listening to him. He got people to participate. The secret to successful strategy for an uncertain future out of our control is *not* to leave it in the hands of a single person. Not even a small group for that matter. It is rather, on a broad basis, to involve those who are expected to implement that strategy. By approaching strategic thinking with the mind of a fox; incorporating a diversity of experience and opinions through conversation circles; and recognising that other players will influence your line of attack, because business is a game, it is possible to design a far more robust strategy for the extraordinary times that face modern business than conventional techniques allow. Furthermore, it is easier to execute the strategy on account of the buy-in already obtained from the executives involved.

We wouldn't have continued the fox analogy in this book if we were not able to enhance it considerably. Over a period of three years since the publishing of our last book, we have had feedback both encouraging and critical. We have listened and taken note. At first we thought that our matrix would need a little fine-tuning. However the opposite was true. We realised that it needed a fundamental reassessment. The prototype was designed to put scenario planning on the map by integrating it into the normal decision-making process. We wanted to convert scenario planning from a fairly esoteric, intellectual discipline into a methodology that was practical, down to earth and considered relevant by the average line manager. We succeeded. But in the process we discovered that the 'game' metaphor was even more powerful than scenario planning in unleashing people's imagination.

So we adapted like foxes to this new insight. The result: a model for a strategic conversation, and how to plan for extraordinary times. It is logically divided into two phases:

A Defining the game; and
B Playing the game.

Defining the game (and the changes taking place in it) lays the foundation for playing the game and deciding on tactics. Despite this being eminently logical, it remains a fact that many businesses still rush into the game without first doing their homework on what the game is about. Imagine the Arsenal and Chelsea soccer managers laying down the strategy for a Premier League clash if the two teams were still hazy about the rules. Similarly, any company that employs a strategy without properly understanding the nature of the game it is in cannot operate effectively. As such, part of the competitive advantage for any company lies in its ability to understand the game better than its competitors.

The first phase – defining the game – comprises five steps:

1. Scope of the game
2. The players
3. Rules of the game
4. Key uncertainties
5. Scenarios.

The second phase – playing the game – also has five steps. They combine the strategic insights gained in the first phase with a more focused view of the possibilities ahead:

6. SWOT
7. Options
8. Decisions
9. Measurable outcomes
10. The meaning of winning.

This ten-step model for a strategic conversation can be illustrated as in *Chart 7*.

The conversation model is anything but a conventional linear model. For one thing, every step is interconnected; and secondly, given the advantages of conversation circles presented earlier, the direction of the process is circular, i.e. a con-

Chart 7 ***The Conversation Model***

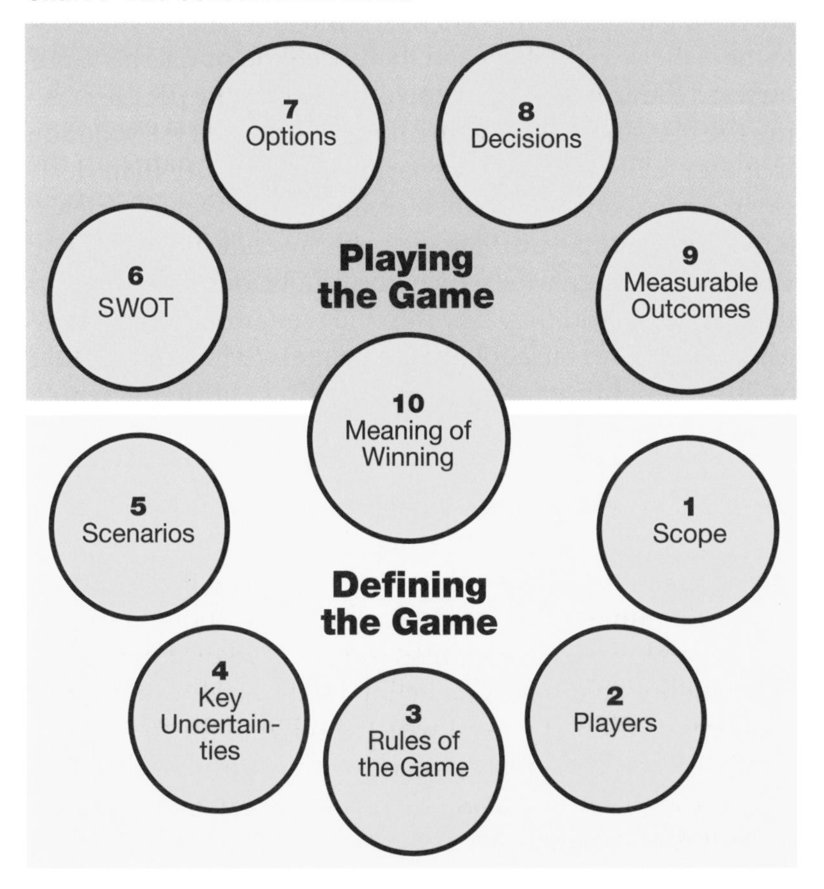

clusion reached later on in the conversation can lead to a review of earlier material. A critical point to note is that our model differs markedly from standard scenario planning methodologies that turn on the insights of a group of scenario specialists from outside an organisation. They interview the executives, hold meetings with them, but then quite independently put together the scenarios. These are fed back into the corporate team who review them and, if they are happy, formulate strategies around them. By contrast, implementation of the conversation model from start to finish involves the decision-makers who contribute all the material to the exercise right there and then. Scenario purists have put forward the argument that you cannot have the people making the decisions also writing the scenarios, on the grounds that they will only write scenarios which justify their decisions. They won't breach their comfort zone. Our experience is exactly the opposite. Management can come up with some very extreme scenarios which pose enormous challenges to the business. And they buy into the scenarios because they *wrote* them. The consequence is an empowering process that builds a capability for strategic thinking within the whole team.

Our approach also makes provision for the immediate noting down of issues for potential action (IPAs) at any stage of the conversation. Standard strategic procedures tend to see them being suppressed or brushed aside until the very end. The programme is too rigid to accommodate thoughts out of sequence. However, we see IPAs as a core part of any strategic conversation, because if no action takes place as a result of the conversation, it wasn't worth having in the first place. IPAs arise spontaneously as each member around the table goes through a moment of self-revelation (aha, this is what we must do). As such, they provide valuable insights into the challenges facing the company and avenues for innovation. In fact, it has often been the case in sessions that we have facilitated that some of the best ideas come out of the blue. We encourage this randomness of thought, as it is very much in step with the words of the philosopher Isaiah Berlin on foxes: "[they] pursue many ends, often unrelated and even contradictory. Their thought is often scattered or diffused, moving on many levels, seizing upon the vast variety of experiences". The logistics for capturing IPAs are dead simple. We keep a separate flip chart or board to capture them in order that they may be reintroduced into the conversation at the appropriate moment, i.e. when discussing options and decisions. The following diagram, that looks like a robot from a Star Wars movie, shows how IPAs can be treated.

Chart 8 ***Strategy to Action***

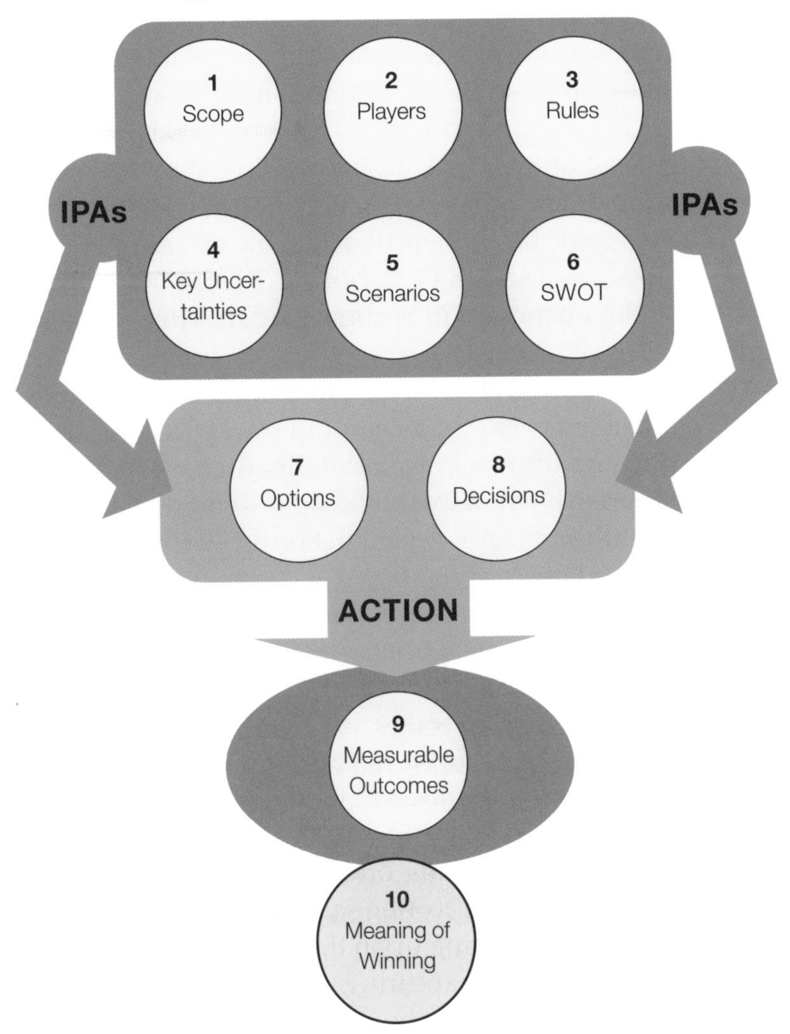

When we undertake facilitation work, we are inevitably asked whether, before any strategic conversation can take place, it is necessary to define the purpose of the organisation. This is a common misperception. Any attempt to define an organisation's purpose at the front end will have the effect of restricting the parameters of the conversation to an area within the purpose as it now is perceived. But how can one tell whether the purpose should or should not be amended until you have examined the context in which the company is operating? In reality, a more accurate picture of the purpose of an organisation will emerge *towards the end* of a strategic conversation. Using our conversation model, it makes sense to close in on purpose in step 10, when the meaning of winning for the organisation is identified. Before that, a 'feel' at best for the purpose will become evident after steps 1, 2 and 3.

We know that we will never convince hedgehogs of the validity of our views. They will want to start with a purpose and simplify the universe around it. But then we believe in the foxy approach whereby purpose may end up being defined in a number of ways, depending on the perspective each person brings to the conversation. For purpose in business is open to a wide variety of interpretations (unlike rugby where the team runs onto the field to score more points than the opponents).

Even more fascinating is that, on a personal level, an individual's 'purpose' as measured by actual behaviour may differ from his or her expressed purpose. Here is an exercise we often use to explain this point. Take a plain piece of paper and divide it up into four sections that represent your personal purpose – family, business, friends, recreation. Depending on an ideal balance of your physical, emotional and intellectual resources, your expressed purpose may look something like in *Chart 9*:

Chart 9
Balanced Personal Frame

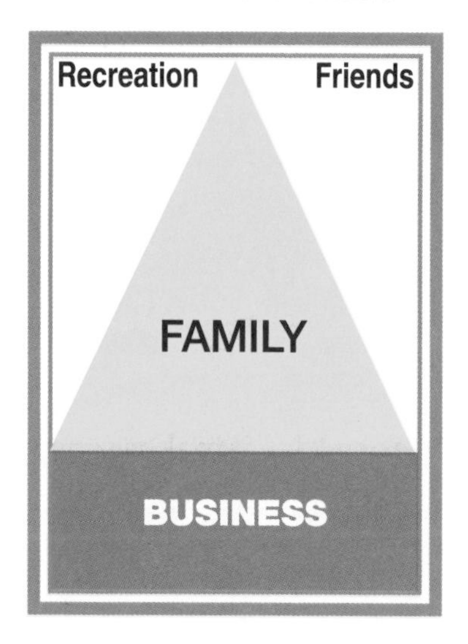

Chart 10
Unbalanced Personal Frame

Business as the source of income for the family is represented as the stable foundation. Meanwhile, the family lies at the centre of the frame, with recreation and friends also being given plenty of space. Now, hand on heart, be honest with yourself. Given the everyday pressures of earning a living and trying to balance family concerns with business demands, your picture of personal purpose may actually look more like *Chart 10*.

Indisputably, this is a horribly unbalanced personal frame. After all, we are called human *beings* and not human *doings*. Nevertheless, as a reflection of the way more and more people live, it is uncomfortably close to the truth. In his book *The Seven Spiritual Laws of Success*, Deepak Chopra talks of one-pointed intention that is "unbending in its fixity of purpose". He goes on: "There is total and complete exclusion of all obstacles from your consciousness." Alas, if the obstacles include putting a reasonable amount of time aside for family and friends, you can end up a spiritual disaster. Thus, one-pointed intention gives us a really prickly feeling!

Similarly, today's modern business has to balance its central interest of generating profits with other concerns such as sustainable development and social responsibility. Ideally, these three items could be expressed in a company's purpose in the form delineated in *Chart 11*:

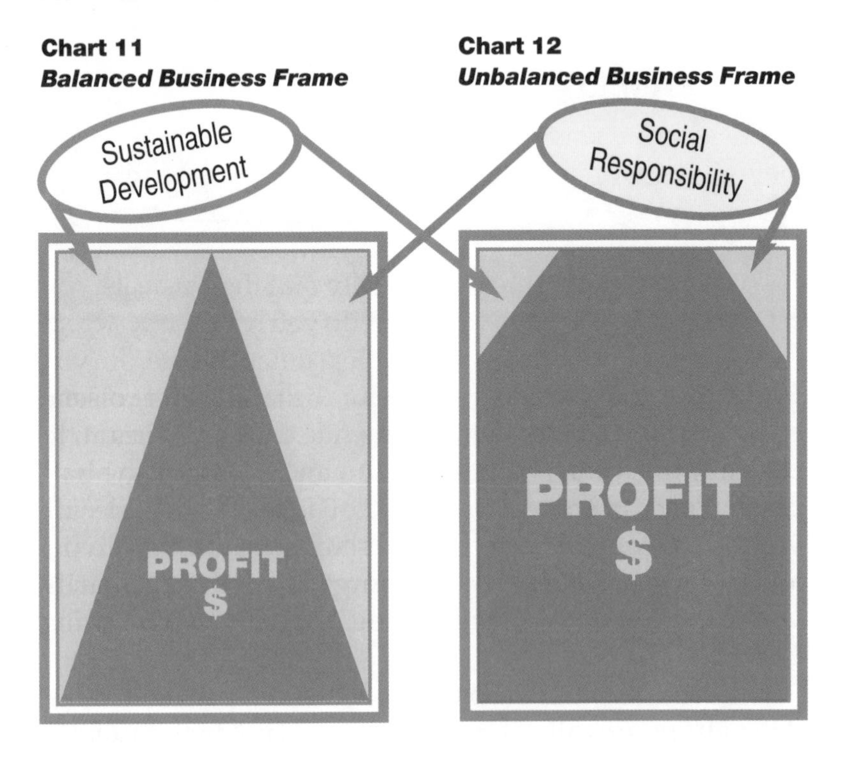

Chart 11
Balanced Business Frame

Chart 12
Unbalanced Business Frame

Sustainable development and social responsibility can be seen as curtains being pulled back to display the profit on centre stage. We like to call this work of art: *Impressions from the Annual Report*.

However, given the unwavering demand of shareholders for a superior financial return, and given that the CEO together with other members of the top executive team usually have sizeable share options themselves, the in-house business purpose can realistically be drawn as in *Chart 12*.

This work is titled: *By Actual Resource Allocation*. It describes the amount of energy, time and money that, if measured, is in truth spent by the executive team on the individual elements of the 'triple bottom line'. As you can see, sustainable development and social responsibility are little more than hooks upon which the profit is hung. It is no coincidence that people who work for companies with an unbalanced business frame tend to be in the unbalanced personal frame themselves, working ungodly hours for the almighty buck. The employees of one institution guilty of this practice referred to it as the 'empty wheels' syndrome. The hamsters get so exhausted that they eventually quit their wheels.

Does this strike you as wrong; or do you reluctantly accept that it is part of winning the game? In a different vein, are you going to comply in a grudging way with the wider role expected of business in society today i.e. do the minimum to pass muster; or are you going to work towards the balanced business frame in *actual fact*? The only way to decide is to have a strategic conversation which concludes with a debate over the meaning of 'winning'. It won't necessarily lead to consensus, but it might result in the company living less of a lie.

The appalling loss of life from the Asian tsunami of 2004 should put everything in perspective. We live on this isolated ball in space which occasionally becomes a very dangerous place to be. When calamities happen, it is desperately important that we exhibit exactly the kind of qualities which are normally crowded out by our desire to advance our careers or make the company grow. If we join hands, we can survive even the most dreadful experiences. If we don't, we shall lose the game now and forever.

The scope of the game

The fascination of shooting as a sport depends almost wholly on whether you are at the right or wrong end of the gun.

P.G.WODEHOUSE

In Africa, much is made of the so-called 'big five', comprising the lion, the elephant, the rhino, the leopard and the buffalo. It is assumed that they are the animals most people want to see when game viewing, and this is why they are singled out and grouped together. The assumption is not entirely true. The last one – the buffalo – doesn't really capture the imagination of most game viewers; it's the other four that people want to see. So why is it in the 'big five'? The name is in fact a hunting term given to the most prized game trophies. A buffalo is right up there with the others because of its bellicose and unpredictable nature – a real challenge to any hunter. Even the lion, the so-called 'king of the beasts', will give a wide berth to a grown buffalo. The two enjoy a simmering degree of respect for the other's power and position within the pecking order. A lion is no match for a fully grown buffalo, but a buffalo calf would be fair game for a hungry lion. Yet, if you were to score animals on a game-viewing outing according to their appeal and accessibility, a buffalo, as a member of the 'big five', would score more than an impala but not nearly as much as a lion. So it all depends on context as to how you rank a buffalo. Context is where the whole game begins.

The same is true for business. It is crucial for any organisation to contextualise its position and performance by examining how it sees the game it is in. Questions should be asked about the type of game that is being played; the nature of the game and its boundaries; and where the organisation

Chart 13 ***The Conversation Model – Scope***

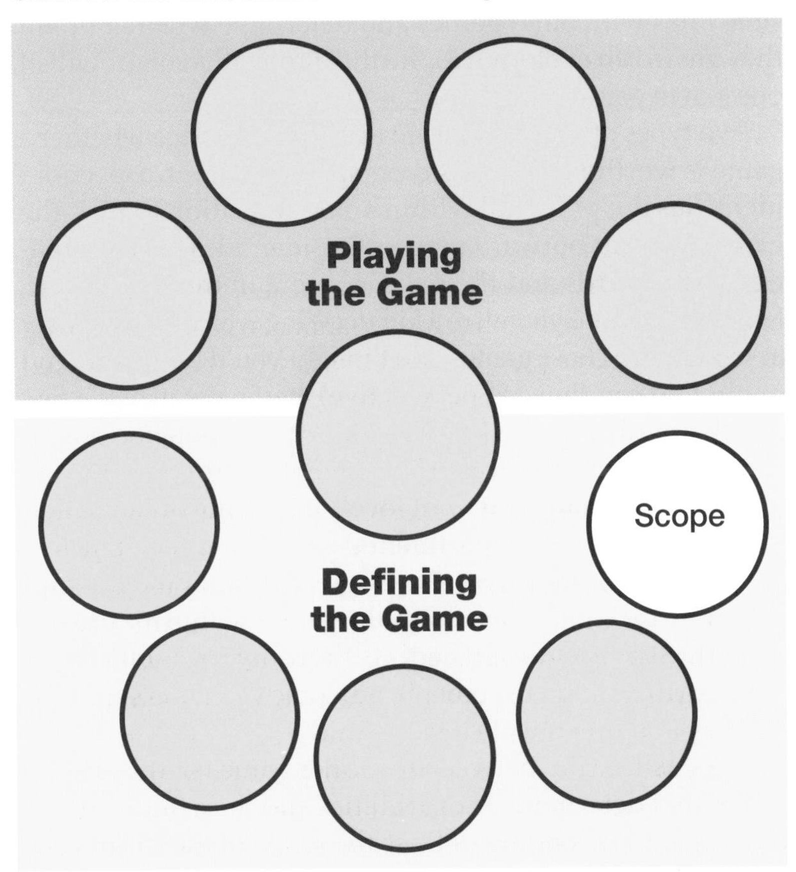

fits into the game as a player. Interestingly, unlike sport which is played on a field or court of a predetermined size, the game of business has no boundaries outside of the constructs of its players, and can therefore be as broad or narrow as they wish to make it. Equally, within business, there will always be links between the games being played by the different sectors. Think of any major project and the number of different companies involved in its feasibility study and commissioning. They play separate games but come together for the project.

A player's talent therefore includes the ability to identify possible links with other games and determine whether or not they are worth exploring for further innovation or growth of one's own game.

Two types of perspective are necessary to judge whether a game is worthwhile. Inward perspective (or introspection) identifies the potential within an organisation to play the game, whereas outward perspective identifies the possibilities, the rewards and the risks inherent in the game itself. Remember when you were a kid deciding which sport to play at school. You chose games you thought you'd be good at and might find fun (inward perspective), having watched a few matches and examined the rules (outward perspective). It is slightly more complicated in business where games are being played at many different levels inside the organisation – divisional games, departmental games and the games of the individual employees. No organisation should attempt to play an external game unless the games within the organisation are sufficiently aligned, i.e. the company is playing as a cohesive team. On the other hand, some variety in skills and outlook is a prerequisite too.

The relationship between the inner games of the organisation that determine its capabilities and the external game it plays in the economy defines the scope of the game – the balance between potential and possibilities. The scope changes according to circumstances outside and direction within. The merger between two companies, for example, may increase their combined potential and therefore extend their range of possibilities and scope. Or the synergies may be outweighed by a clash of cultures which diminish possibilities and scope. Associations or partnerships with players in other games may expand scope. On the other hand, a bad management decision may damage a company's reputation, devalue its stock price and hinder its future scope.

To repeat what we said at the beginning, the gameboard upon which a company plays is defined by the company itself. Identifying scope as a starter in a conversation is designed to encourage participants to confront what they think is obvious – "We make widgets for watchamacallits and damn fine widgets they are too. Just read the mission statement in our Annual Report. What else do you want?" This is what they like to believe, but is it true? In examining the scope of the game in which the company operates, it's similar to evaluating the *fish:pond* quotient – is the company a big fish in a small pond; a small fish in a big pond; a growing fish that is feeding on the smaller fish in the pond; a complacent fish in an increasingly polluted pond; an ageing fish in a changing pond; or a floating guppy in a fishbowl about to be flushed?

It also makes sense to kick off with scope because it is familiar territory that people can move into straightaway – it encourages a participatory environment. It is seemingly innocent. If we were to represent the scope of the so-called 'big five', we could simply take a photo of them, together or separately. But how can we 'capture' the scope of an organisation in a conversation? Imagine that you had an empty frame in front of you and you had to fill it with a picture of your organisation – not of the buildings and the staff, but a representation of its operations. What would it look like? Within the framework of the industry it is in, how does it feature? Does it have a national presence or even a global presence? These are some of the questions that need to be asked in identifying the scope of a business.

The elements of scope – the balance between potential and possibility – can be represented in three diagrams: the Picture Frame, the Seven Frames and the Looking Glass. Before we continue, it is important to remember that none of these frames has a rigid content. The latter may be refined or revised as a result of any strategic conversation in any year. One in a million may be like the enigmatic smile of the Mona Lisa, which will remain forever the same! Moreover, we do not mean you to use *all* the visual aids we have inserted in the rest of the book literally. Many of them should act as 'prompts' to conversations. In the end, it is up to you to decide in what way you want to employ our diagrams.

An organisation is defined by the type of business area it is in, the activities it performs in that area and the nature in which it plays the game. The Picture Frame represents a picture or a snapshot, the frame being the operational boundary of the organisation, and the space inside being the current scope of its business and activities. Expressed in one way, the picture could contain all your core businesses with the more important at the centre and the others radiating outwards in order of significance to the organisation. Non-core businesses you want to sell would lie outside the frame altogether. Likewise, activities undertaken by the organisation to produce its goods and services can be split into core activities at the centre with the more peripheral ones towards the outside. Activities you are likely to outsource, because they are either a drain on the company or no longer form part of the core competence, would similarly lie outside the frame. We promise that just this analysis alone excites an animated discussion.

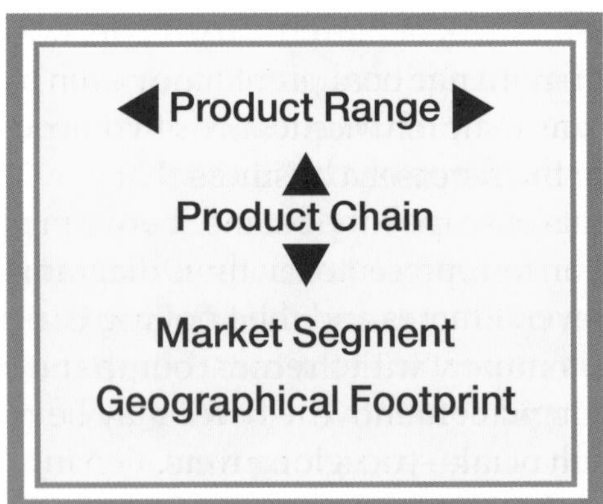

Chart 14 ***The Picture Frame***

However, the strategic conversation only really takes off when you start asking what you want the picture to look like in five to ten years' time. How different do you want it to be, if at all? To assist with this part of the debate, we have divided the picture into four components: product range (which covers both physical products and services), product chain, market segment and geographical footprint. As can be seen from the diagram, we regard product range as equivalent to horizontal diversification and product chain as equivalent to vertical integration. Examples of questions that should be asked include the following:

Product Range

What is your product and service range? (For those starting out, what is it to be?) Do you want to widen the range to achieve more diversification? Do you want to narrow it to achieve more focus? Do you want to keep it the same? Is the attention of top management too widely dispersed or appropriately concentrated? Is the mix of your products/businesses right? Do you want to change the mix in light of market trends or greater intensity of competition? Are there any businesses in your portfolio that are not core to your product range? Do you want to sell them? Are there any new products that can be organically developed from existing core competencies? Have you any products in the pipeline that constitute a step change because of innovation? Can you add services such as maintenance to any of your physical products and thereby increase your range that way?

You may also wish to recycle some of your products for environmental or commercial reasons. Obviously, if you want to change your product range radically, you may have to take over another company with the core competencies in the area into which you want to move. Growing those competencies from scratch may take you a long time.

Product Chain

In your industry, what are the processes that make up the production (or value) chain from the ground to the customer? In which ones are you represented? Do you want to go further upstream to control your inputs or go further downstream to capture value closer to the customer? Are there missing links in the chain where you might wish to develop core competencies? In which part of the production and marketing chain do you think you are strongest and in which are you the weakest? In the latter case, are you forming alliances or joint ventures with other companies more specialised in the relevant fields? Should the range of functions currently performed in-house stay the same, or should more of them be outsourced?

Some companies, such as oil companies, like to be represented in the entire chain (in the case of oil from the well to the petrol pump). Others like to stick to a link in the chain and dominate it nationwide (retail chains) or worldwide (fast-food chains).

Market Segment

Is your current market growing or diminishing as a result of changing demographics? Where are the best opportunities to expand? Do you want to broaden your customer base with new products aimed at different income and age groups? Should your marketing campaigns be suitably modified? Or might there be a downside to the exclusiveness or timelessness of your brand? Are you too dependent on a specific industry or company for your sales, and should you be looking for other clients?

Geographical Footprint

For each step in the process defined so far, are you adequately represented in terms of geographical footprint? Are there other cities, states or countries of interest to explore in terms of marketing to them, establishing businesses in them, or both? Are you sufficiently diversified in a geographical sense so that no city, state or country can impact on your results too seriously if that city, state or country goes through harsh times, or is global reach a bridge too far?

So, how's your *fish:pond* quotient now? Fancy other ponds?

Manchester United Football Club is an example of a company – now listed on the stock exchange – that has grown way beyond its traditional scope – the game of football. From this core it has moved into the merchandising and retail game. It sells many products which are dependent on the brand being successful. Thus, the irony now is that should the football side suffer a losing streak, the merchandising and retail game will pay the penalty. The real game (of soccer that is) impinges on the business game. Moreover, with the worldwide explosion of broadband technology, Manchester United is on the verge of entering the broadcasting business. It is expected to be amongst the first football clubs to broadcast all its matches on the internet in real time in an effort to reach a subscriber base of 'displaced supporters' around the globe that number in the millions. So what conclusion do you draw? The club has to keep on winning!

The concept of using pictures as part of the strategic process is, we agree, somewhat unusual. Nevertheless, we would argue that evaluation through graphic representation is a powerful and enlightening tool. Child psychologists will often turn to the artwork of young children to get an idea of their issues. These pictures are not assessed on the artistic accuracy of their components but rather on their proportion and relationship. Questions would be asked about how and where the child represents herself in the picture. Is she standing next to other people in the picture or is she on the outside? Who in the picture is larger than the others? Where are lines of contact and where is there representation of emotional disengagement? And, more importantly, is she smiling?

So, even though we don't want you to take our diagrams too literally, it is worthwhile to ask how the yardsticks used by child psychologists can be transferred to the corporate world. Well, it can be done by giving executives a plain piece of paper, and asking them to draw a picture frame like the one we showed earlier; then fill in the picture with their representation of the organisation and the game it is in. Not every manager is a Monet, so the product may consist of simple line drawings, a sequence of shapes or sketches, or even a written picture, depending on their level of artistic skill. For example, an accountant may find it very difficult to draw anything that does not involve numbers – and we've all seen how creative some accountants can be with these! On the other hand, some groups will draw the company's annual report – creative indeed! It's a revealing exercise, as it gives a first indication of how the organisation thinks. The most important strategic insight gained from this exercise is whether the organisation has the imagination to grow in conditions which it least suspects. The more impressionistic the drawings, the more likely it is that it can.

The next diagram – The Seven Frames – places a company in the context of other games played outside and within it. There are always games within games or, as our diagram shows, a bigger picture behind a smaller one. Moving inwards, one should evaluate the role of the company in the internal sub-games being played inside it. The question here is: how much should a company interfere in its internal games? Similarly, how much should a government interfere in industry or corporate games? Where should a line be drawn in terms of interference, because not all interference can be considered negative? In soccer, a manager is expected to interfere when the team goes off at half-time to the dressing room. He will give them a piece of his mind if they're losing and encouragement if they're winning. However, if he continually shouts orders from the sideline during a match, he may confuse them at best and demoralise them at worst. So there's good interference that encourages innovation and team spirit, and can help win the game; and bad interference which creates animosity and frustration instead of alignment. Balance is sometimes hard to achieve if a team has a hot-blooded manager, a company has a hands-on CEO or a country a dictatorial leader.

Chart 15 ***The Seven Frames***

You will recognise the middle frame as the one we drew for the company in *Chart 14*. In relation to this, the inner frames represent the games that go on inside the organisation, i.e. the games played by each business unit and department, as well as those played by individual employees (remember the balanced and unbalanced personal frames unveiled earlier). Clearly, you need some alignment between all these games in order for the group as a whole to function as an effective entity. But where do you draw the line between centralisation and decentralisation so that you get everybody 'singing from the same hymn sheet' (a phrase beloved by CEOs) without killing entrepreneurial spirit?

Another implication of the diagram is that the CEO should receive a summary of the strategic conversations undertaken by the business units, because he or she will simply not have the same level of knowledge of the game as the people who play it every day. This applies particularly where the game is being played in another country which has unfamiliar rules. The perception of the players living there is crucial to future investment decisions by the holding company resident in a foreign land.

The outer frames represent the increasingly larger and more complex environmental games within which the organisation must play – those of the industry as a whole, as well as national and international games. Sustainable development can only be achieved through a correct balance or alignment between the organisation's inner and outer frames. An excessive concentration of focus on the inner frames will lead a company to become increasingly out of touch with the realities around it; whereas directing too much energy towards the outer frames might result in your falling behind your leaner and meaner competitors who keep to the basics of a strong game in-house. Yet, ideally, all seven frames should be aligned through a common thread. In a way, it's similar to the concept behind the popular *Where's Wally?* books. In the latter, a cartoon character called Wally is hidden amongst a myriad of other similarly coloured characters, with the object being to find him. Each page represents a different time or place in history, but the common thread is a hidden Wally. In business the concept goes beyond the simple game of finding a character. It is to do with building an understanding of context and continuity – both essential for ensuring sustainable growth. A successful organisation is one that directs its energies along a path that weaves between the internal (organisational) and external (environmental) frames, revisiting them continually to achieve a competitive edge in the wider and narrower game. This interface between the frames is the true scope of the organisation – the balance between its internal potential and external possibilities.

An example of the importance of this balance can be found in the scope of the banking sector in a developing economy like South Africa. The inner frames of the banks naturally concentrate on solving the paradox between creating a customer-centric model and streamlining their organisational and operating structures to bring down costs. However, performing this egg dance on its own misses out on the bigger picture. For, in order to play the game properly in a developing economy, the external frames of the banks should be sending them signals on the need to assist job creation and encourage entrepreneurial start-ups. Besides expanding their client base, initiatives in this direction will help create an inclusive economy with a viable middle class bent on preserving stability. The result: a more sustainable national game and greater value for the banks in the longer run.

For similar reasons, it makes sense for a multinational company to have a conversation around the Seven Frames for each of the countries within which it operates. The national frame in each case qualifies as the context of the company's operations there. If the rules of the game for the company are not aligned with those of the national frame, then the company has two options: change its own game to suit the local game better or get out (obviously, where corruption is the name of the game, it's preferable to get out). Each national game is different. Cultures and social customs – the unwritten norms that help define the rules for each national game – are varied and complicated. One man's burp is another man's compliment.

Equally, multinationals need to understand the international game in order to play effectively across borders. All those GATT and World Trade Organisation rules, all the potential stuff to come out of the Kyoto Protocol on global warming, all the regional rules like those imposed by the European Union on anti-competitive behaviour, need to be examined as part of the outermost frame. The conditions set for these games are way beyond the control of any multinational to influence. Their only choice is to comply (though some mount hugely expensive legal challenges which are normally fruitless). Consequently, it goes without saying that alignment needs to be secured if all the picture frames are to fit. And this is as true of the frames pointing inwards to the employee as it is of those which point outwards to the world at large. But alignment can be derailed through glaring mismanagement or through the most noble of intentions. Take individual performance bonuses. Managers driven by such incentives may well abandon any ideas of teamwork that might dilute their reward. In the same vein, business units or departments that are driven by performance-based incentives may form silos that exclude the involvement of other units or departments. These actions can cut across alignment to the extent that the company loses the overall game. So beware!

During the part of the conversation when an organisation is considering scope, a critical self-analysis has to take place at the same time (to match internal potential with external possibilities). Hence, the inclusion of the Looking Glass, so that you can take a long, hard look at yourself in the mirror. Later on, it will help you identify strengths and weaknesses; in the latter case any gaps between your current potential and the new opportunities afforded by expanding the scope of the game. Your options will then include actions to fill the gaps. To help you get a feel for your reflection, we have inserted six elements in the Looking Glass.

Chart 16
The Looking Glass

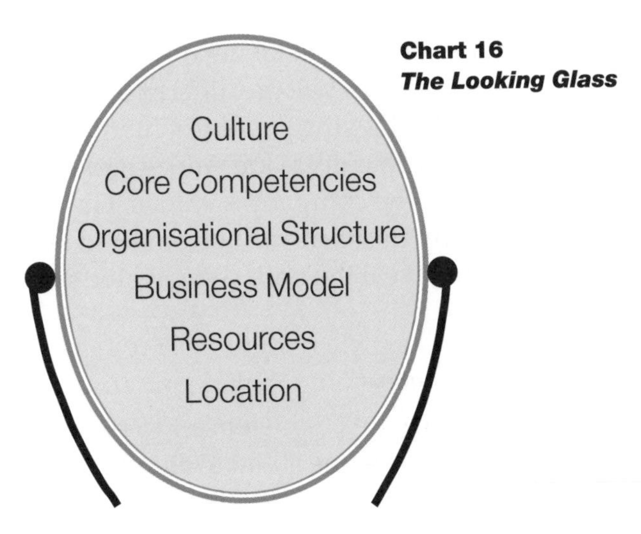

The kind of introspective questions you should be asking yourself are:

Culture

In describing the scope of my game, is the culture existing in my company at the moment the best one to win it with? If I'm a multinational, how do I cope with the cultural differences between my workforces in different countries, and how do I superimpose some form of corporate identity that welds them together as a cohesive team? Where I am expanding the scope either to include other products or other steps in the product chain, is the culture materially different in these new areas? For example, in the mining industry, exploration demands a far more entrepreneurial culture than managing mines to exploit the deposit. Elsewhere, retailing demands a completely different culture to manufacturing and wholesaling. Does my remuneration structure encourage the kind of culture which I believe is suitable for the industries that I'm in? Where I'm selling into a new market segment, e.g. younger consumers, how will I change my culture to appeal to them? If I'm thinking of taking over another company, will our cultures merge, or will the differences be perpetual stumbling blocks to achieving genuine synergies?

Interlinked with culture are values and similar questions can be asked of the company's values. However, ethical issues are already raised at various points in the conversation which tend to reveal the underlying value system inside the company.

Core Competencies

Do I possess the core competencies to play the game as it is played now? Is the game about to change to the extent that a completely new set of competencies will be required? Is my training and development programme geared to produce the requisite core competencies in each of the countries I'm operating in, and do those countries have adequate feedstock coming out of their education system? If not, where in the world am I going to obtain suitable recruits? If I am extending the scope of my game, can I do it organically by building on my core competencies so that I can spread them into the new areas? Or will I have to acquire them by forming some form of commercial partnership / relationship with another company? If I'm stepping out of the frame into a completely new product or business, do I grow the skills from scratch myself inside my own company? Or do I approach candidates holding senior executive positions in other companies who I know already possess those skills, and – should I secure their services – let them build new teams around them? Do I look around for a suitable takeover target and do all these things at once?

Organisational Structure

Is my organisational structure correct for the game I'm in? If the game is evolving, is my structure evolving along with it? As with a soccer team, should I be changing the arrangement of the players on the field to get better results? Is my structure too flat so that I lack sufficient control? Is it too hierarchical so that it makes for clumsy and slow decisions? Where I am entering new games, what is the structure of my competitors and should I emulate it? If I am about to widen my geographical footprint, will I need to move from a centralised to a more decentralised structure?

Business Model

Is my business model robust enough to cope with all the scenarios that my existing game can produce? How will I have to amend my business model if I am entering new games or new countries? How much flexibility should I build into my business model to cope with the variations of doing business on different continents? What are the differences between my business model and those of my competitors? Do the differences give me a better chance of winning the game? If not, how am I going to change my model?

Resources

In terms of the relative importance I attach to the games I have identified under my scope, does my allocation of human, financial and other resources reflect my priorities? Should I be concentrating my resources on a narrower front to defeat my competition (normal war strategy), or should I be acquiring more resources in order to achieve a better standard of performance in the various games I am playing? Should I be cutting back on overheads in order to release money so that I can have more troops on the ground? Or should I be making total cuts just to be a lighter, tighter fighting force overall? What could these retrenchments do to staff morale? Where I am contemplating other games, do I really have the resources to enter them, especially if they are much bigger games? If not, where in the market will I obtain these resources?

Location

Where is the present centre of gravity of my operations and where will it be in ten years' time? Should I be moving my head office now so that it will tie in with my future geographical footprint? In order to play the game most effectively in each of my host countries, in which city is it best to have a local office and principal representative?

In ending this section, we would just like to point out that any general worth his salt asks all these questions before he commits his troops to battle. The Looking Glass is very much part of developing military strategy after the scope of the battle (terrain, enemy numbers and disposition, weapons) has been estimated. However, given how much the nature of the war game has changed in the last twenty years, one must ask whether governments have gone through the same process of logic in equipping their defence forces for current rather than obsolete threats. For this reason, we normally warm up the discussion on scope by seeking a preliminary opinion on how the nature of the game has changed in recent times and how it might change in future.

Players

All the world's a stage,
And all the men and women merely players.
WILLIAM SHAKESPEARE

Unlike chess, which has two players, business has to contend with many players (frequently referred to as stakeholders). We are most interested in those who can have a significant

Chart 17 ***The Conversation Model – Players***

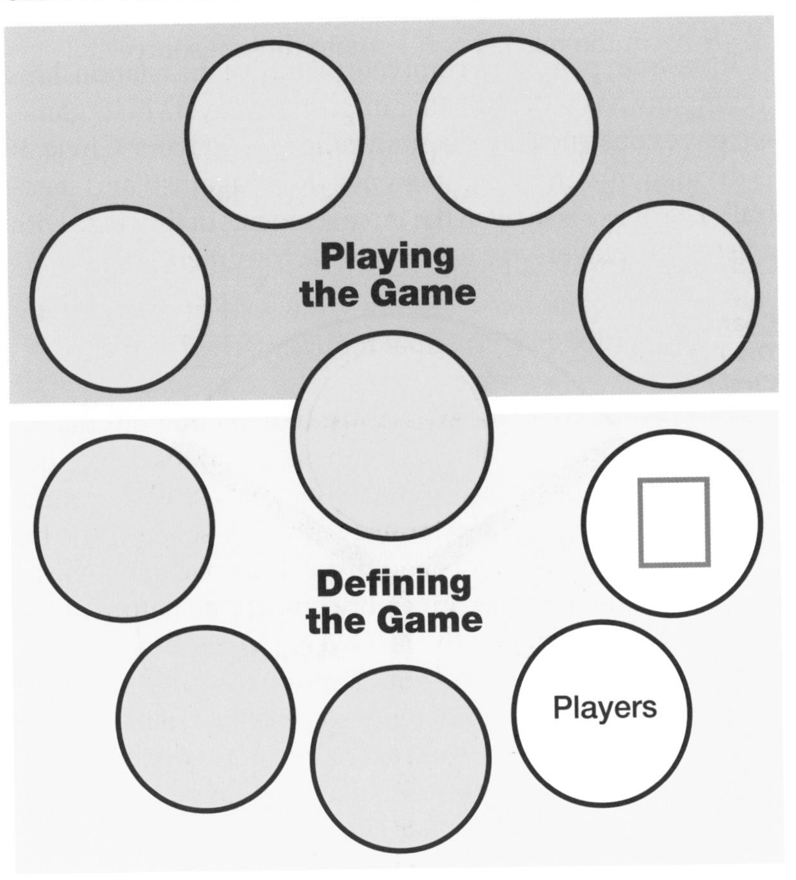

impact on the bottom line. To keep to the sporting analogy, if you are to win, you need to know as much as possible about the people playing in the same game. Understandably this includes both those players on your side as well as those in the opposing teams. In terms of business strategy, however, we have included a third category: players who are neutral. It is best to think of neutral players as 'poised' between the two camps. In other words, under certain circumstances, they could be 'for' you. In other circumstances, they could just as easily be 'against' you. Sometimes, they are genuinely 'neutral'. It depends where their interests lie at any moment in time.

To assist in painting a complete picture of the relationships a company has with the other important players in its game, we have constructed a diagram called the Players' Circle. It is divided into three components: 'for', 'against' and 'neutral'. The object is to fill in the three segments of the circle with a list of the players appropriate to each segment.

Chart 18
The Players' Circle

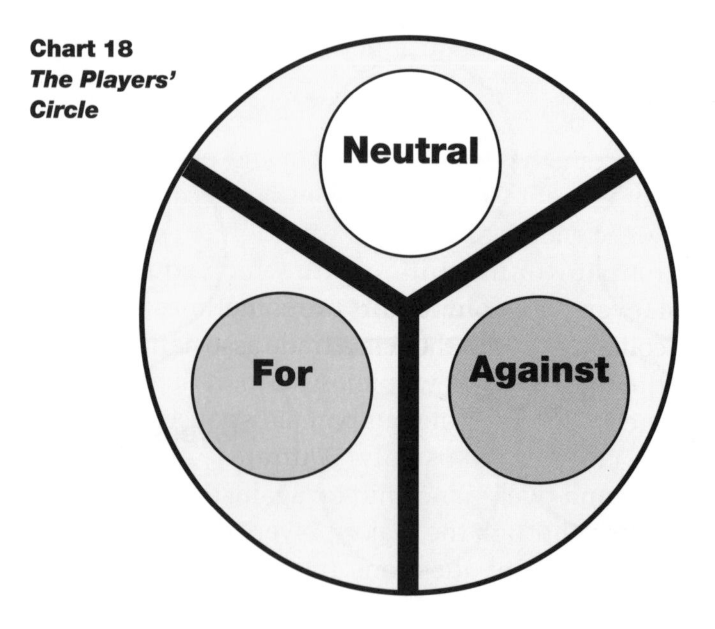

In conversations we facilitate, we are frequently asked to clarify exactly what we mean by the three categories. Do we mean by 'for' that the player has a positive/supportive relationship with the company, or that the player actively assists in increasing the bottom line? Likewise, does 'against' mean a negative/destructive relationship, or that the player actively seeks to diminish the company's bottom line? Does 'neutral' mean independent like a referee or, as we have already suggested, sometimes for and sometimes against? The answer is that life is never simple and it depends on the player under consideration. For example, competitors are always against you in our terminology because, while they may respect you, they want to win the game as much as you do. You're battling over the same turf. Suppliers can be 'for' you when you have established a positive relationship with them over time – even though they are going to pursue their own interests up to a point in the annual price negotiations. It depends how reasonable they are and how much they value your relationship. Obviously, if they try to use a dominant position in the supply chain to gouge the maximum price out of you, you would put them in the 'against' column. The same will apply if they offer your competitors discounts which they don't offer you; or if they don't deliver on time; or if they regularly break other conditions of the contract because of wilfulness or inefficiency. It's all a matter of judgment where you put each company or institution with which you have an interaction (even your competitors are sometimes 'for' you when you collaborate with them in a trade association which promotes the industry as a whole). And then there is your family. Where would you put your parents, spouse, children? For example, children are usually 'neutral' as infants, 'for' between three and twelve and shift to 'against' as teenagers!

Let us now go through the major players in business and provide some pertinent questions and comments on each.

Competitors

Who are your real competitors, the ones you go head to head with? You should identify them by name. What are their strengths and weaknesses compared to yours? So many companies do a SWOT analysis on themselves, but never swot up on their competitors. Maybe it's vanity! You would have thought such an exercise would be an elementary first step in plotting strategy. After all, the first thing a tennis player at Wimbledon does before facing his opponent on court is to watch videos of his opponent's previous matches to see if he has a weak forehand or backhand or can't volley at net. He adjusts his strategy accordingly.

Then there's the relative size of your competitors compared to you. Do they qualify as 450-pound gorillas while you weigh in as a mid-sized orang-utan? Can they threaten you with economies of scale which you will never hope to achieve? The red lights should be flashing if you are starting to become a troublesome itch in their side. They can swat you to death. Maybe it's time to quit the game or else tie the knot with one of the gorillas. Jack Welch once said that you have to be No. 1 or No. 2 or fix, sell or close your business. He's not absolutely correct, because you can be highly differentiated and survive in your own niche. BMW is neither the No. 1 or No. 2 global car manufacturer, but it makes a tidy profit.

Perhaps it's the other way round and you're a Goliath surrounded by nimble Davids with greater agility and lower overheads than you. Remember, a swarm of bees can kill you! Sometimes in an industry there's a whole bunch of small guys out there operating in the informal zone who can outmanoeuvre you with special deals and sell at half your price. They (and their hives) must be taken into account.

Then what about all your indirect competitors who may not be in exactly the same sector as you but who are competing for the same buck? If you're in jewellery, what about all the other luxury goods manufacturers? If you're in air travel, what about all the other forms of transport? You don't have to make a list of all the companies in the category 'indirect competitors', but you must bear them in mind because any change in their status for better or for worse may have a profound impact on your game.

Suppliers

Suppliers can fill any of the three segments depending on your relationship with them. It's tragic how many suppliers have no understanding of their customer's game and vice versa. The relationship is basically adversarial and founded on ignorance – neutral to negative. IT companies in the 1980s and 90s were in the habit of selling systems to customers, which were far too exotic for their needs. They were doing nobody a favour. They were only thinking of their own game. On the contrary, suppliers should be helping you to win *your* game, not theirs. Today, supply chain management is the new slogan. To make it real, you should be sitting down with your suppliers not just to hassle over prices on an annual basis but to gain an understanding of each other's games (and maybe adjust the contract to suit both sides). Then you can move to the 'for' column in each other's circle. Again a SWOT analysis of your key suppliers is no bad thing, because you inherit all their strengths and weaknesses, opportunities and threats as a lower member on the food chain.

Customers

When did you last do a customer survey to ascertain what customers think of you? If you're in the middle of the product chain, what do the end-consumers think of you and your product? Come to think of it, what do the public feel generally about you? Many world-class companies take it for granted that brand excellence is a perpetual thing and their customers can automatically be placed in the 'for' column. Not so fast – if it's an assumption you should check it out. Independent surveys give you the brutal, honest facts. Don't rely on hearsay. It's worth recalling that your customers may be 'poised' to use one of your competitor's products – in which case they are in 'neutral'.

Employees

Would you believe it, but we've had the executive teams of companies put senior management in the 'for' column and employees in 'neutral'. That's a strategic issue, if ever there was one! Greece won the second most coveted soccer trophy in the world in 2004 – the European Championships – not because they had the most talented individual players, but because they had the *best team*. Your employees are your team and if they are in 'neutral', you are hardly likely to win your industry's premier trophy in any category. In today's networked business environment, you often hear the phrase "your people are your assets". Though the expression is becoming hackneyed, it is nevertheless true. The public want to know that you are a decent employer and put your money where your mouth is.

Trade Unions

Where labour forces are unionised, trade unions are important players in the corporate game. When labour relations are good, trade unions are usually put in the 'neutral' column; but when they're bad they go in the 'against' column. Obviously, the latter is a drag on the business and is at the very least a strategic issue for the human resources director.

Shareholders

Like soccer fans, shareholders are usually 'for' you if you are doing well and 'neutral' to 'against' you if you are doing badly (depending on whether they perceive the cause to be a tough external environment or bad management). Shareholder support can be crucial during crisis periods. It therefore confounds common sense how many board remuneration committees go out of their way to anger the shareholders by granting the CEO plus his top sidekicks unreasonable pay hikes in bad times. The financial community, including pension fund managers, stockbrokers and financial analysts, are not amused either.

Where a company has a major shareholder, the relationship can have a huge influence on the destiny of the company. It's always interesting asking subsidiaries what their opinion is of the holding company (having promised it will never get back!). In one case, the subsidiary put its holding company firmly in the 'against' column on the grounds that the latter consistently vetoed all capital project proposals in order to maximise dividends out of the company.

Sometimes it's not nice being a cash cow. You can be milked to death.

Government

Most companies put government in 'neutral', which is where it should be as a neutral referee. Occasionally, it is put in the 'against' column if it has just levied a burdensome tax increase on a particular sector or made life more difficult in another way. Multinationals must of course consider the governments of all the countries in which they have operations as players. The relationships with these various host governments may differ dramatically, calling for changes in the geographical footprint if problems in a particular country can't be overcome. On the other hand, where governments are consistently put in the 'for' column by big business, they can be accused by their opponents of 'crony capitalism'. Nevertheless, building a strong relationship with government and demonstrating a long-term commitment to the country are, in many cases, the passport to successful investment by foreigners.

Communities and NGOs

With consumers becoming more discerning in their choice, having communities and NGOs in the 'for' or at least the 'neutral' column is becoming increasingly a factor in winning the game. Have you ensured with all your projects that local communities have participated throughout the feasibility phase? Have you set up corporate social responsibility programmes around your operations which make a sustainable difference to the quality of life of impoverished people in the vicinity? Are environmental impact assessments on your projects conducted by neutral, independent bodies? Otherwise, NGOs can really bite you if they are effective watchdogs. And so can quangos and gongos. No, they are not mythical beasts like griffins. They are quasi-nongovernmental organisations and government-organised nongovernmental organisations. Essentially hedgehogs in disguise!

Media

We've left the fourth estate to last, but don't underestimate what a powerful player it can be. The relationship, if good, is usually 'neutral', because it is built upon a healthy tension. They want sensational stories and you need to be in a position to negotiate that sensation to your benefit and not at your expense. The most critical question to ask yourself is this: if something really nasty happens, have you got a contingency plan in place which not only corrects the problem but handles it honestly and openly? The first 24 hours after an incident can make or break a company's reputation for a very long time. Cover-ups lose you the game.

So when do relationships with any of these players become

elevated to the extent that they qualify as strategic issues? The answer is when your ability to play the game is severely impaired because the relationship is not in the right part of the circle. Moreover, you may have to abandon the game if something is not done to improve the situation. Relationships with competitors will always be adversarial, and therefore their strategies count as much as yours in the final outcome of the game. You can out-strategise them; you can take them over to convert them from 'against' to 'for' (except that cultural differences often undo the good of any merger); or you can just slug it out together in the local market and look for fresh opportunities overseas (preferably in territories where your competitors are absent).

Conversation around players is also important when there is the need to negotiate a major contract. This type of analysis will give you the chance to identify the players with the greatest value in the negotiation process. It will also allow you to assess whether they are likely to start in the 'for', 'against' or 'neutral' column. As the negotiation proceeds, you can plot their change of position. Your final objective may not be to win the game per se, but to ratify an agreement in which all parties consider they are winners. These agreements tend to last longer than the win-lose variety.

To add to the challenge, one of the effects of globalisation is player complexity – there are more players than ever before and their influence over the game has become increasingly diffused. We ultimately live in one world where the value of meaningful relationships is the true measure of competitive advantage. The secret to winning the game lies in the ability to build relationships and then use them as leverage to enhance your position in the game. But let's not get sentimental. There are no friends in business, only those with shared interests who are momentarily willing to play your game because it is also theirs.

We'd like to end up this section with a bit of wisdom and humour. When one of us was facilitating a session for a church recently, we had almost completed the list of players when someone asked: "Where would you put God?" "In neutral," replied one of the priests. "Really," said someone else, "I thought God was on our side." "That's the problem," responded the priest, "Everybody thinks God is on their side, whereas God is on everyone's side." Game, set and match to the priest.

Rules of the Game

How would you like it if you were a business executive
and when you made a mistake, a red light
went on and 18,000 people started screaming?

JACQUES PLANTE
Canadian ice hockey goal tender and the first player to wear a mask in a game

Every game has its rules, but they are not always set rules like those given on the inside of a *Scrabble* box. The rules of life are more subjective – more like parameters as perceived by each player. Even moral rules are subject to different interpretations, particularly when it comes to exceptions. Rules may be influenced by the players, such as in a game of 'tag' being played by children, or they may be determined by forces or factors outside of the control or influence of the players. Laws of government and corporate codes of conduct fall into the first category, the forces of nature and principles of science into the second. T.H.Huxley, a nineteenth-century English scientist, put it thus: "The chess-board is the world; the pieces are the phenomena of the universe; the rules of the game are what we call the laws of Nature. The player on the other side is hidden from us."

Some rules don't change, such as those in chess, where the

rules have remained unchanged since the game originated in India in medieval times. However, in business there is only one rule that doesn't change, and that is that the rules of business vary in different locations and are always changing (wherever you are). They change from culture to culture; from country to country; they change through developments in technology; and they also change as a result of social and political events. They can also literally change overnight.

Broadly speaking, the rules of any game include both writ-

Chart 19 ***The Conversation Model – Rules of the Game***

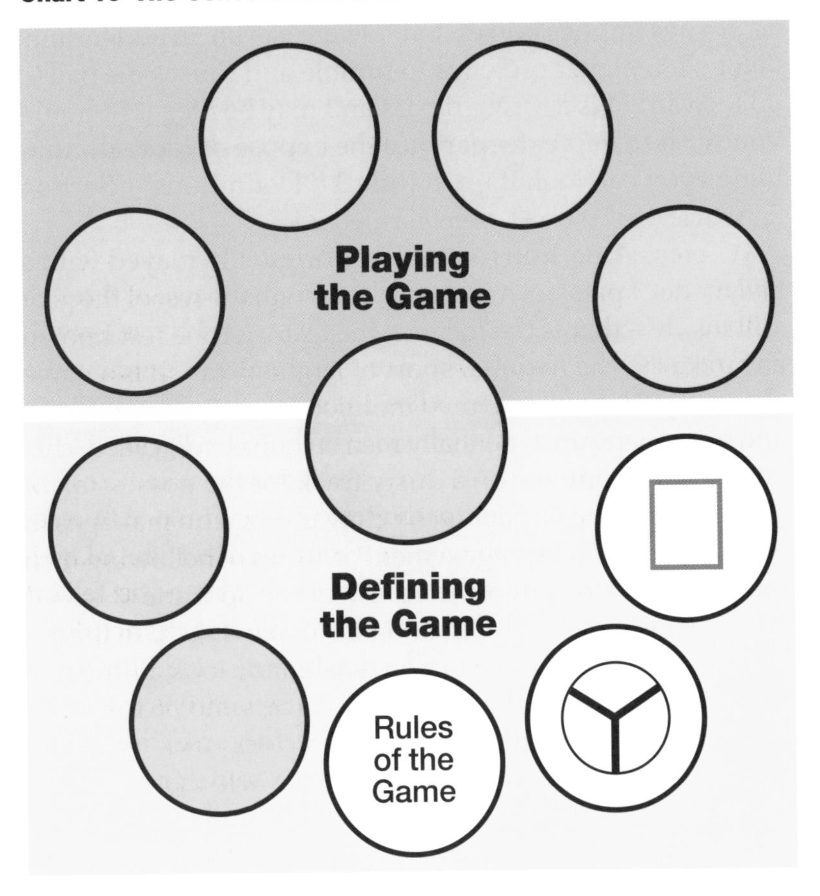

ten and unwritten rules, and the difference between them is very important. As an example, let's compare two national sports – one in America and the other in Afghanistan. When it comes to sport (and their constitution), Americans, it is well known, are very particular that rules should be written down. They should also be specific and preferably complex. Apparently, paradoxically, this makes them easier to apply. Take for example the game of American football, as governed by the National Football League, that rules a 'fumble' as the following: " . . . any act, other than a pass or legal kick, which results in loss of player possession. The term *fumble* always implies possession". There's even an addendum: "Note: If a player pretends to fumble and causes the ball to go forward, it is a forward pass and may be illegal." Should you wish to delve deeper into the exposé of football fumblings you can look it up in Rule 3 ("Definitions"), Section 2, Article 4, of the NFL official rulebook.

Whereas American football was originally played with a ball made of pigskin, it is a goatskin – with the rest of the goat still inside – that is the focus of the testosterone test known as buzkashi, the national sport of Afghanistan. It is a game shaped by the time-honoured tradition of recognising courage and horsemanship. Essentially men on horseback (called 'chavandozlar') compete on a dusty track for the possession of a dead goat. The winner is the chavandoz who manages to evade the crunching engagement of scores of bellowing men on horseback, to gallop around a marked spot and to speed across a line whilst still clutching the hapless goat. To the average American football fan buzkashi may look a little like pandemonium played with a goat's carcass and no rules; but it is in fact a game with very strict *unwritten* rules regarding qualification to play and behaviour on the field that have been handed down via word of mouth over hundreds of years, and enforced through social debate, physical squabbling and the occasional beheading. Some may argue that it sounds rather uncivilised, and yet fail to see the similarities with one of its derivatives – polo.

So, whether written or unwritten, all games have rules. This is essentially and unequivocally a determining factor in the nature of any interaction between people, and between people and their environment. Remember those videos that were played backwards on the TV programme *America's Funniest Home Videos*? They were funny because in real life you don't see riders who have fallen off their horses into a puddle, and are covered in mud, immediately jump back on their horses all nice and clean. It breaks the rules. Even heavy metal music has rules because it is music of sorts. But to return to our sporting analogy, if you are aware of the rules of a particular sport and as long as you do not break them, everything else is fair game; and that is the area in which you can freely exercise your interpretation of the game and operate to your advantage. These rules may be comprehensive and explicit as in the game of American football, but the game of business is more buzkashi than Superbowl. Some of the rules are predictable (like tax and company law), everything else is not; and it is this unknown area that represents an exciting array of untapped possibilities.

The rules of any game in life are therefore an amalgam of written and unwritten rules that have been put in place by a host of governing bodies including schools, governments and sports administrators. Then there are rules that have been introduced by the players themselves, and finally there are rules that have just come about through changes in the market or the environment with no human intervention whatsoever. All these rules may or may not change over time.

Just as there are rules that determine the relationship between animals – such as where you stand in the food chain, e.g. lions trump the rest – the rules of business, as viewed by the business community, will determine whether a company survives in the corporate jungle. Recognition of these rules is paramount, because they shape the genetic blueprint of the game – its DNA. We therefore call them the *descriptive, normative and aspirational* rules of the game. Woe betide anybody who doesn't examine them before deciding on strategy.

Descriptive rules, as the name suggests, describe the basic rules of your market, i.e. what in your estimation is predictable about it. For example, you may be in a declining market, a growing market, a market becoming increasingly competitive, a market that is going to be more / less regulated, or one where the opposition is consolidating into larger business enterprises. They embrace any contractual arrangements limiting your sphere of action including agreements with parent companies, licensing conditions, treaties and informal deals with third parties. Descriptive rules also determine a company's basic *licence to operate* in the countries (or regions like the European Union) where it does business. These include legislation and tax codes, but more importantly the 'unwritten rules' that govern business relationships. It is these rules that often differ from country to country. Here is a selection of unwritten rules from one Far Eastern country: sign the contract and then the negotiation begins; if you cause someone else to lose face, you lose face yourself; and when driving, anything behind you is of no consequence i.e. *what ifs* you spot in your rear-view mirror are too late, so don't torture yourself.

Two critical questions that should be asked around descriptive rules are: have there recently been any changes in the descriptive rules which could affect any part of your business and are there likely to be further changes?

A good example of a recent change in these rules is black economic empowerment in South Africa. You need a BEE in your bonnet to operate here. No question. The top executive team can also *make* rules which give a company its corporate identity. These rules are then handed down to each department as descriptive rules of the game. They cannot easily be challenged.

Normative rules are the *moral rules of the game* to which any world-class company has to subscribe to keep its world-class badge. You don't have to be a rocket scientist to list them. Honourable people know them off by heart. They are your conscience. They are the rules that, if adhered to by a company, demonstrate a noble sense of purpose that the public respects. Break them and you lose the badge of honour in a nanosecond. Normative rules include those on corporate governance and SHEC (safety, health, the environment and the community). In the military lexicon, they are normally called the 'rules of engagement'. Such rules are universal in the sense that they are valid across the world (unlike descriptive rules). Where a company applies different standards in this sphere, the fact is immediately picked up by the media, with the offender being publicly castigated.

Yet, for many companies driven solely by the quest for increased profits, normative rules of the game are at best tolerated. But this is a risky game because minimal compliance can so often lead to individual employees flouting the rules with fatal consequences.

Important questions that should be addressed at this point of the conversation include: Are there any new normative rules in the pipeline in host countries? Which countries in the world can be ruled out of bounds because the company cannot operate there according to the normative rules it has laid down for itself? Company values are the backbone for the normative rules of the game and should therefore be made explicit at this stage. No gifts, no thick brown envelopes, no commissions via intermediaries, no lowering of standards in Third World countries, no disparities in working conditions, no creative accounting, etc. People will soon get the drift: foxes can become quite hedgehog-like over values.

Aspirational rules are the *rules to win the game*. What are the aspirational rules for each step of the process and for the business as a whole? Answers might include management focus; branding; other forms of differentiation to make your product/service unique; cost leadership; maintaining an entrepreneurial flair; attracting, developing and retaining talented young people; a perpetual spirit of innovation (both incremental innovation to achieve operational excellence and radical innovation leading to a change in the game you play); and understanding the rules of your customers by forging long-term relationships with them. Without being biased in any way, we can give you a great example. Fox News, a cable TV news network in America, differentiates itself from the other networks by being quintessentially American, openly supportive of the Administration and covering major domestic stories (such as high-profile murder trials) in considerable detail. It has made large inroads into the market as a result. Aspirational rules of the game can be equated to the value drivers of the business. They should create commercial value in the game and enhance the ability for survival and growth. A company's 'vision' can often be developed from the aspirational rules, as they constitute an understanding of the meaning of winning the game.

The importance of knowing and understanding the rules of the game cannot be stressed enough. But here's the twist: there is no complete set of rules for any game at any one time. Because each game is influenced by the actions of the entire roster of its players, every game is continually changing. If it didn't change, all the rules would become known and the game would cease to evolve. Therefore the most effective player in any game is that player whose understanding of the rules of the game is closest to the 'real' permutation at that moment. In other words, they may not 'know' the game, but they have a better 'feel' for the game; and are in a better position for 'intuitive' decision-making.

In a way a game and its combination of rules is like a lottery with a permutation of, say, ten numbers, and where part of the combination of numbers, say six of them, remain pretty constant. Furthermore, some companies know more of this set combination of six numbers than others. The payouts are incremental and shared equally amongst those with the same correct numbers. The company that wins is the one which knows all six of the set numbers and then gets, say, a seventh and an eighth one right. But then the first and maybe the second of the set of six numbers may change because of the change in strategy of that one company. Everyone then has to re-evaluate the game plan. And so it goes on.

Some markets are so tight and business is so competitive that a detailed conversation about the rules is a prerequisite for any degree of competitive advantage. Moreover, some changes in the rules are so deceptive that they could be missed unless there has been an upfront conversation about them. Yet so many companies play the game in wondrous oblivion of the rules, let alone any changes in them.

Through their continual evolution, the descriptive, normative and aspirational rules of a game exist in a continually shifting yet balanced relationship that can best be expressed in the form of a triangle:

Chart 20
The DNA Triangle

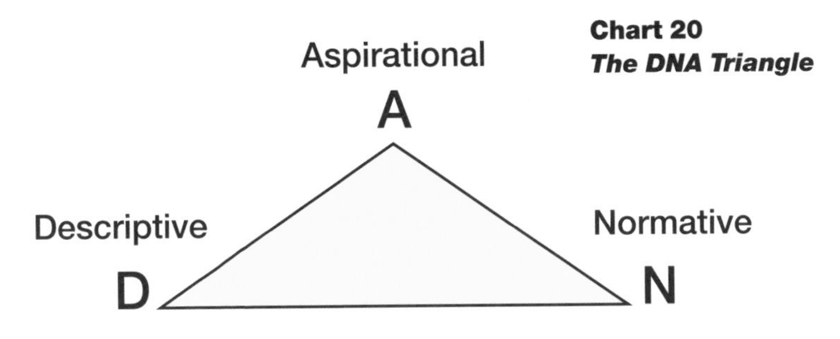

The descriptive and normative rules for a game are located at the base of the triangle and the aspirational rules at the apex, because the aspirational rules can't be achieved unless the descriptive and normative rules are fully complied with. Any company that wishes to be sustainable acknowledges this. Moreover, companies that fail to achieve the aspirational rules are encouraged to 'get back to basics': to revisit the descriptive and normative rules and examine whether or not they are being followed.

Similarly, just as some animals thrive under certain circumstances and not under others, depending on the fit of their genetic make-up with the environmental conditions around them, so too are some companies better aligned with the DNA of a game by virtue of its being compatible with their own inherent character and temperament. Sometimes just the very conversation in a company around a game's DNA is enough to throw up anomalies in the company's compatibility with its environment, which may explain why the company is struggling vis-à-vis its competitors. Like a polar bear is better suited to arctic conditions than a brown bear, a company with its roots firmly planted in a particular industry and steeped in its culture is better equipped to handle the future than a relative newcomer. On the other hand, if the newcomer is a fox, it may have spotted a change in the rules which turns the industry's DNA upside down and makes all past experience irrelevant. Indeed, a revolutionary fox often induces the changes in the DNA of the game in order to favour the newcomer.

Hence, any company that really wishes to move from good to great has to be a fox, *not* a hedgehog (foxes eat hedgehogs). You have to be constantly alert to changes in the rules of a game, some of which may be sudden and explosive, some gradual and subtle. Furthermore, you have to lead the pack in your response. Examples include rules that were aspirational (such as those governing social responsibility and environmental concerns) that become normative or even descriptive rules. Any company that doesn't comply with these rules is now out of the game. Similarly, unwritten rules sometimes become written rules. Many world-class companies understand this and respect and adhere to unwritten rules before they are written down in the statute book. In other words, resourcefulness covers pre-emptive action as well as creative response. This doesn't mean that in order to be successful one must concentrate on adhering solely to the descriptive and normative rules of the game at the expense of the aspirational rules. It is a temptation, particularly when faced by a highly regulated business environment. However, any attempt by a company to regulate its own game by constructing too many written descriptive and normative rules runs the risk of distorting the game and limiting its entrepreneurial spirit and capability for innovation.

Of course, no company can exist on its own. It is part of a chain which stretches from the raw materials supplier to the end consumer. Each part of the chain has its own DNA rules. This relationship can be illustrated as in *Chart 21*.

Chart 21
The DNA Chain

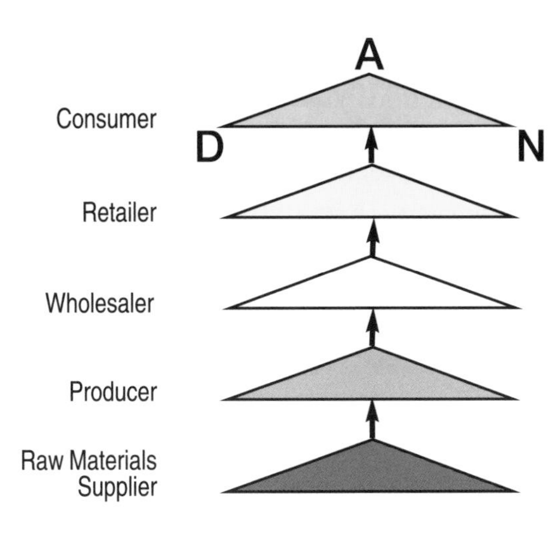

Nevertheless, for a chain to be effective there needs to be some DNA alignment between its constituent parts – some common themes pervading the chain as a whole. If any part of the chain ignores, say, the normative rules of the game, it can threaten the stability of the entire chain. For example, if it was found that a subcontractor to a leading brand of sportswear was using child labour in the manufacture of its element in the chain, human rights lobbying groups would be quick to call for consumers to boycott the final product. The damage to the brand and its raw material suppliers and retailers could be substantial. This relationship becomes crucially important when parts of the supply chain are in different countries. Each of the latter may have different descriptive rules, but double standards – as we've already remarked – are a killer.

If the supply chain is not aligned, it can destroy real value. Antagonism between the links weakens them. There has to be value on the table for everybody in the chain. Unfortunately, where huge imbalances in negotiating clout exist between players in the chain, this principle is thrown out. One joke doing the rounds in the farming community in Wales goes like this: "What is the difference between a terrorist and a supermarket? Answer: You can occasionally negotiate with a terrorist!" If your company is smart, it will conduct conversations with each player in the supply chain to understand the DNA rules of their game and, vice versa, they can understand yours. Where there are inconsistencies or contradictions, they can be mutually ironed out. The chain stays intact. The same, of course, applies inside a company where different departments have different DNA rules. For the production process to be smooth and efficient, every department has to have an understanding of the other departments' needs and rules.

In today's increasingly networked business environment,

we ought to shift away from viewing a supply chain as a long line of sequential service providers to one of interconnected partnerships through a widespread building of relationships. This building of relationships can only take place if, in the process, it creates value for each player in the network. In turn, the player adapts his or her role to optimise the output for the network as a whole. Because players have the best knowledge of that part of the game they are contributing to, and the associated rules, an effective network will entail regular conversations amongst all players to generate a working knowledge of the network rules coexisting alongside their own rules. This builds a common understanding among the players, so that if rules pertaining to the overall supply chain change, a team solution can easily be provided.

Furthermore, the concept of networking recognises that in the same way as different players make up a single supply chain, so every player is connected to *other* supply chains, each with its own DNA rules of the game. This increases the complexity of any game for your average networker, but that's how it is in today's interdependent world. You have to be all things to all people. The result looks a little like *Chart 22.*

Chart 22
The DNA Network

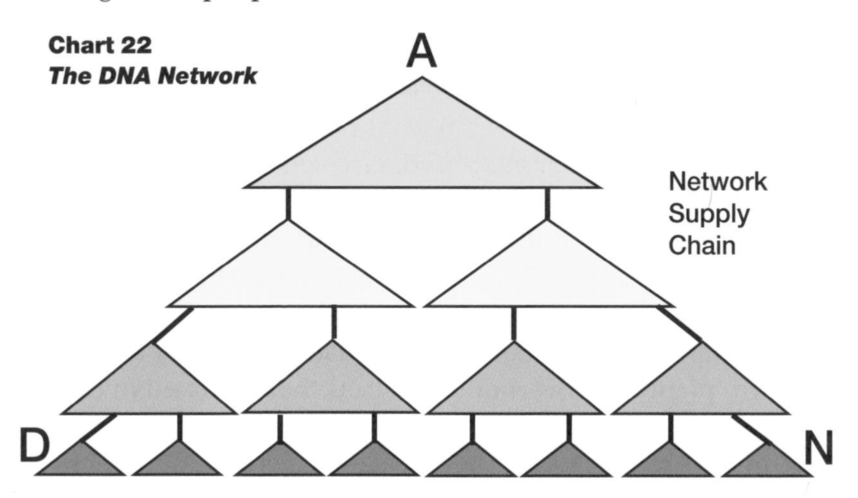

The network supply chain demands a wider degree of alignment within its various components than a single supply chain. Equally, each individual chain within the network has its own unique DNA rules, demanding flexibility from players at the intersection of the chains. Any misalignment results in the loss of value, any misidentification of which chain you're in does the same. So, it's a lot more complicated than the business model of only fifty years ago.

With all these written, unwritten, descriptive, normative and aspirational rules of the game that emerge through conversation, as well as the demands for compatibility in interpretation of these rules amongst all the players within the greater supply chain network, you could be forgiven for thinking there's more out there that is unknown and out of your control than you first realised. You still want to be a hedgehog? You're kidding! If you were playing this game like a fox you'd factor these complexities into your strategy as best you can. You'd play business chess.

Key Uncertainties

I wouldn't give a fig for the simplicity this side of complexity, but I'd give my life for the simplicity on the far side of complexity.

JUSTICE OLIVER WENDELL HOLMES

Chess masters would not be where they are if they did not study in advance the characteristic moves of their fellow players and future opponents, as well as their playing style and temperament. Yet, when they face each other over a chessboard, plenty of uncertainty exists as to the pattern of play. Even though the scope of the game means it is played move by move and the possibilities for each move are limited, there

Chart 23 ***The Conversation Model – Key Uncertainties***

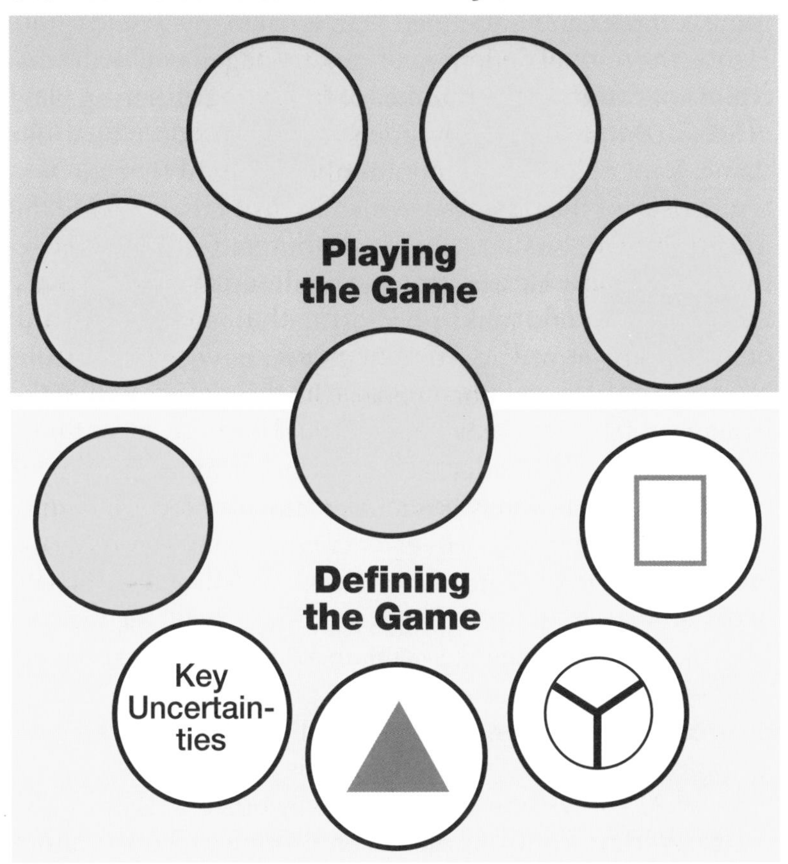

are still degrees of uncertainty surrounding an opponent's overall strategy. One miscalculation on his intended move (which means you make the wrong one) and you can end up being mated. This is what makes the game of chess so exciting – for those who find chess exciting, anyway.

In the game of business, however, uncertainties for any company are not limited to the strategy of other players in the game, but also include events and conditions that exist within the company and the industry, as well as national and global uncertainties. The game of business is therefore far more complex and undefined than what many would think. Hence, the normal definition of 'risk management' as the discipline of counting the number of fire extinguishers in head office is completely out of touch with the modern business game. Real risk management is about identifying the systemic risks of the business, which in turn are related to the uncertainties a business faces without and within. It is extraordinary how classic strategic planning methods simply ignore this fact and make no allowance for surprises. Think of how many strategic workshops you have attended and how many times risks of a generic kind have been comprehensively debated. We bet not many, if ever.

If one were to consider the sort of uncertainties a company encounters, they may be global, national or local in nature. They radiate inwards in ever-decreasing shells (the closest being local as in right inside the company). Besides this type of classification, they can be grouped into political, technological, economic, legal, social and environmental uncertainties. We have represented these groupings in the form of the petals of a flower, colour-coded according to the geographical arena that the uncertainty is located in.

Chart 24 shows how, in fact, the various petals of uncertainty overlap. For example, an environmental uncertainty can lead to change in technology, which may have an unknown impact on society. The closer the uncertainty is to the central area of the flower, the more sense a company can usually make of it. But it also depends on the size of the company. The local arena is particularly important for small companies, whereas multinationals would place more emphasis on the national as well as global arenas of uncertainty within each petal. Political rulers of countries or regional blocs (such as the European Union or NATO) may need to focus equally on all three.

This is not to say that uncertainties that are global or national in nature will not have an impact on a small company. Remember the seven frames in the scope of the game. The most important consideration in key uncertainties is the word 'key'. Key uncertainties are those uncertainties that can have a major influence on a company's bottom line. They are key in that even though they may seem inconsequential to the untrained eye, in reality they can smack you hard or provide a great opportunity. A single person having a heart attack, for example, may seem insignificant to all but the victim and his or her family, but it could just be that the late, lamented person is a head of state. Imagine if, say, the leader of Pakistan or India meets with an untimely demise, to what extent tensions in the region could escalate and change the nature of political risk. Imagine an assassination like that of Archduke

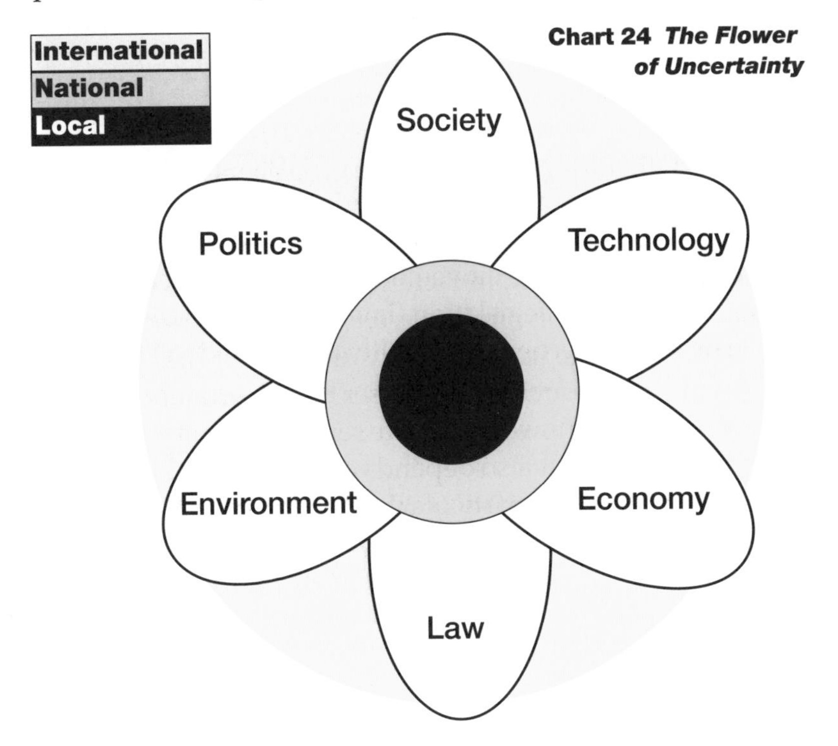

Chart 24 ***The Flower of Uncertainty***

Ferdinand in Sarajevo in 1914 and what that could trigger. On the other hand, man-made or natural catastrophes like 9/11 and the Asian tsunami tend to have a selective impact on business: obviously affecting those companies in the direct path of the tragedy the most; indirectly affecting associated industries like airlines, tourism and insurance; and leaving the rest relatively unscathed.

Examples of key uncertainties within each arena include:

Global

The global economic cycle (economy), international terrorism (society / politics), natural disasters and climate change (environment), shifts in international regulations (law), the price of oil and other forms of energy (economy / technology), base metal, food and other commodity prices (economy), security of supply of raw materials (politics), technological advances and product substitution (technology), etc.

National

The effect of epidemics such as HIV / AIDS (society / economy), each country's economic performance and political risk (economy / politics), consumer taste and demand (society / economy), relative movements of currencies (economy), changes in national legislation (law / politics), trade liberalisation or barriers (economy), quality of road and rail network (economy), etc.

Local

Prices of local labour, goods and services (economy), safety and security (society), education and health facilities (society / economy), quality of local government (politics), neighbouring competitors' strategy and performance (economy), local environmental and community issues (environment / society), diversification of local economy, etc.

Uncertainties can cross over borders. An epidemic can start off locally and then become a national or international phenomenon. A technological shift likewise. Competitor strategy can hit you at any level, depending upon whether the competition consists of small local players, foreign firms or multinationals with local franchises (e.g. McDonald's, Starbucks). Civil war can spill over national boundaries and infect entire regions. Normally the uncertainties an industry faces (as opposed to the company as an individual entity) fall into all three categories. It may well be of value to pigeonhole industry uncertainties in a separate box.

Local uncertainties may also include uncertainties within the company such as the risks associated with declining efficiencies; too little control (theft, corruption, fraud); or too much control (bureaucracy). Added to these are the possibility of accidents causing death, injury or downtime; computer viruses; loss of reputation through unacceptable work practices; and a talent exodus through poaching by competitors. Or there may be an unhealthy level of internal politics or succession issues at the top. It could be argued that the level of these uncertainties can be influenced by decisions within the control of the company (unlike say a global economic downturn or recovery). However, accidents happen within the most sophisticated and carefully prepared endeavours – the space shuttles Challenger and Columbia are perfect examples.

The strategic conversation around key uncertainties needs to be facilitated very carefully. If it is handled properly, it can unlock insights into the kind of circumstances which might change your strategic direction. It can also help you envisage emergency tactics to keep you on course in the event of winds approaching hurricane level. There are no rights or wrongs other than, whatever approach is adopted, it should give people the wings of imagination. The conversation is about stimulating insight into all relevant possibilities and developing a framework in which the implication for the company of each possibility can be teased out. This is no place for being prescriptive about the order of proceedings, as intuition and creativity of thought play a crucial role in the conversation. The outcome may be a random list of key uncertainties on a flip chart. For some companies, that's good enough to move on to the next step of preparing scenarios.

However, we have something more detailed in mind for the purpose of processing the information that emerges from the discussions. We recommend this alternative purely because the experience is so unique and the information generated is like a treasure house. Thus, like gems need sorting, the uncertainties captured should be codified as far as possible according to petal (society, technology, etc.) and arena (global, national or local). They should then be numbered so that they can be plotted on the corporate equivalent of a radar screen, which we will come to shortly. One of the most important reasons for having a radar screen is so that you can continually ask yourself whether or not an uncertainty is turning into a reality and if so whether appropriate contingency plans have been put in place to handle it. In a general sense this concern can be articulated in the following question: Does our company have a sufficient degree of flexibility in its decision-making processes to adapt quickly enough to significant changes in its circumstances?

So how can a company capture these changes on a radar screen and have an idea of the consequences should they materialise? Given that uncertainties are by their nature unpredictable, and that the focus of attention is on their impact on the company, a 'radar screen' will reflect these two key features. We have therefore developed a graph with varying degrees of predictability on the vertical axis and expected impact on the horizontal axis.We call this a Predictability Impact

(PI) Chart. Before going into the chart in detail, we must explain why we chose 'predictability' as the measure on one axis, as opposed to 'probability' or 'certainty'. The reason is that it covers the two sorts of things which we have in mind as key uncertainties for our chart. The one kind consists of ever-present factors like commodity prices, exchange rates or, perhaps, the future of the Chinese economy. You can say that these items are 'unpredictable' because of the dispersion of possible outcomes, but you would never use the word 'improbable'. The second type of uncertainty comprises shock events such as disruption of oil supplies through terrorist attacks, the outbreak of a new epidemic or your company becoming the object of an unwelcome takeover bid. You can state that these events have become more 'predictable' or maybe 'probable', but it would be awkward to remark that they have increased in 'certainty'. It just doesn't sound right and could even convey the wrong impression.

Besides, we must draw another distinction between predictability and probability. The first tends to be subjective in that it incorporates the level of confidence you have in your judgement, as well as the odds of something happening. Probability tends to be impersonal and objective, a mathematical term. The logic goes like this. In a laboratory experiment that is repeated a sufficient number of times, the different outcomes are counted and a probability is attached to them (like spinning a coin gives you a 50/50 split on heads and tails). In real life, you can't repeat things that often so you can't attach probabilities. You can merely take a stab at how predictable something is – not in the sense of giving a specific percentage but rather saying that it is more or less likely or totally unlikely or reasonably likely.

Moreover, although predictability and probability normally go hand in hand, i.e. something that is highly probable is highly predictable, occasionally they part company. Human frailty being what it is, our powers of prediction let us down and something happens which in hindsight was highly probable but we didn't predict it (because we did not have enough information at our disposal). That's how accidents unfortunately happen. The scenario was never played out in the minds of the people responsible. A sound business judgement obviously rests on identifying a threat or opportunity and getting the level of predictability and impact about right. It's as bad to conjure up an obscure risk as a reason not to go ahead as it is to ignore a clear and present danger when proceeding. But the long and the short of it is: don't attach specific probabilities to key uncertainties or scenarios. Otherwise, you may make a fool of yourself by being accused of bogus accuracy. One scenario planner who gave a 65 per cent probability to an event happening was asked by the CEO: why not 66 per cent, why not 64 per cent? What's so special about 65?

In order to start constructing our PI Chart, we begin with a basic truth about uncertainty. One can divide the future into known unknowns and unknown unknowns – things we know we don't know and things we don't know we don't know. We made this distinction in *The Mind of a Fox*. Donald Rumsfeld subsequently made exactly the same point in a memorable quote and was laughed out of court by his opponents and media hedgehogs alike. Too bad for them. Unless a person has supernatural powers of foresight, the list of uncertainties relevant in his or her life will never capture them all. So you have to keep a general level of flexibility in your outlook to handle the unknown unknowns that come at you from 'left field' or, as you can see in our chart opposite, from below the line.

A good example was that Saddam Hussein acted as though he had weapons of mass destruction, when he didn't. He was an imposter who illogically brought about his own destruction (unless he truly believed the Americans wouldn't attack).

Chart 25 *The PI Chart I*

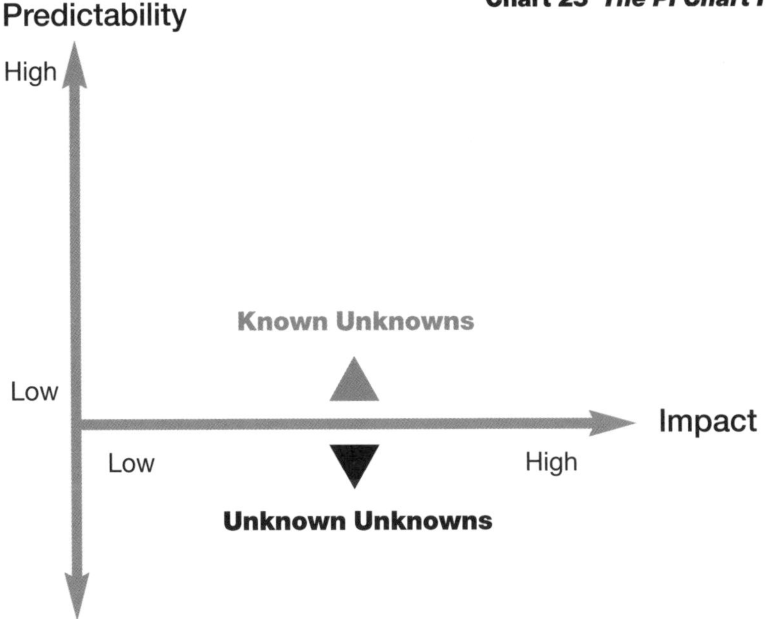

To the British and American intelligence agencies as well as Donald Rumsfeld, his behaviour was an 'unknown unknown'. Equally, to these same people, 9/11 itself probably qualified as an unknown unknown, because they didn't think an Arab terrorist group was capable of organising such a massive attack on Western soil. To many South Africans – particularly those who invested offshore – the recent strengthening of the rand was an unknown unknown. They couldn't believe that an African currency could strengthen against the US dollar. They were wrong! Whenever a paradigm is strong, watch out for the opposite.

By contrast, a known unknown is one we know exists, such as the next earthquake on the San Andreas Fault in California, but whose timing and magnitude are unknown. As you can see in *Chart 26* on page 103, the 'known unknown' uncertainties can be graded on the PI Chart according to their level of predictability. The ones with a very low degree of predictability, due to the absence of hard facts or very low probability of occurrence, we call *wild cards*. Similarly, those which surpass a given and very high degree of predictability qualify as *rules of the game*. By the laws of elimination, the ones left with a low to medium degree of predictability are the ones we define as the *key uncertainties*.

Now the parameters have been set, it's a case of 'plotting' the key uncertainties on the radar screen according to their predictability and potential impact. Let's say, after all the uncertainties were discussed, grouped and numbered, the ten most important were identified and plotted. The completed PI Chart could look like *Chart 27*.

The two uncertainties numbered 3 and 10 are *wild cards*. It is worth keeping an eye on them because, if conditions change, they can turn from blobs on the lower deck into sharp images at the centre or top right. Numbers 1, 2, 8 and 9 require close monitoring right now because of the impact they can have. Perhaps the company can reduce its dependence on the outcome of these factors through some judicious diversification or hedging programme.

Itemising the uncertainties this way deepens the discussion and allows people to debate their significance in more precise terms, and make more sense of the overall risk profile of the business. It also prioritises the company's intelligence-gathering needs. More importantly, it helps to focus and fine-tune the company's strategic thinking in that, once the uncertainties have been tagged, the objective of the company may be to improve its take on the predictability of the event under consideration, reduce the potential impact of the event, or a combination of both. Obviously, some things have an inherent level of unpredictability surrounding them that no amount of analysis can reduce. World GDP growth, the strength of the US dollar, the gold price and the oil price come

Chart 26 ***The PI Chart II***

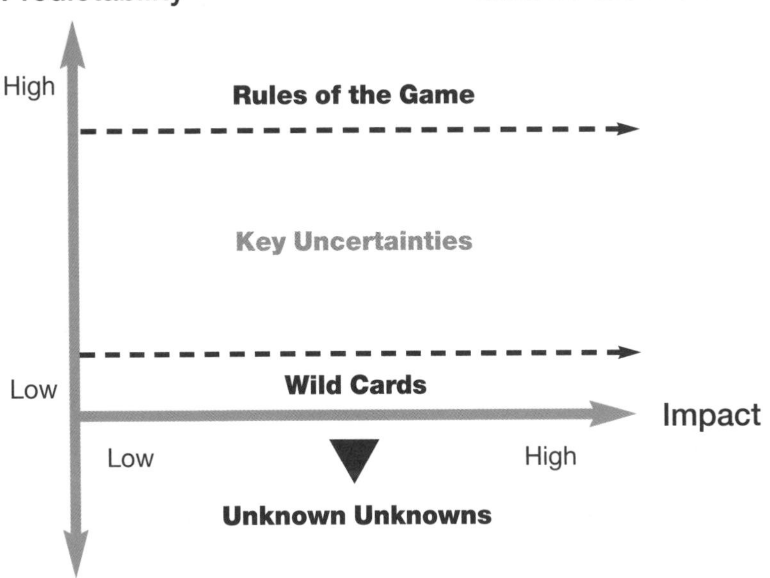

Chart 27 ***The PI Chart III***

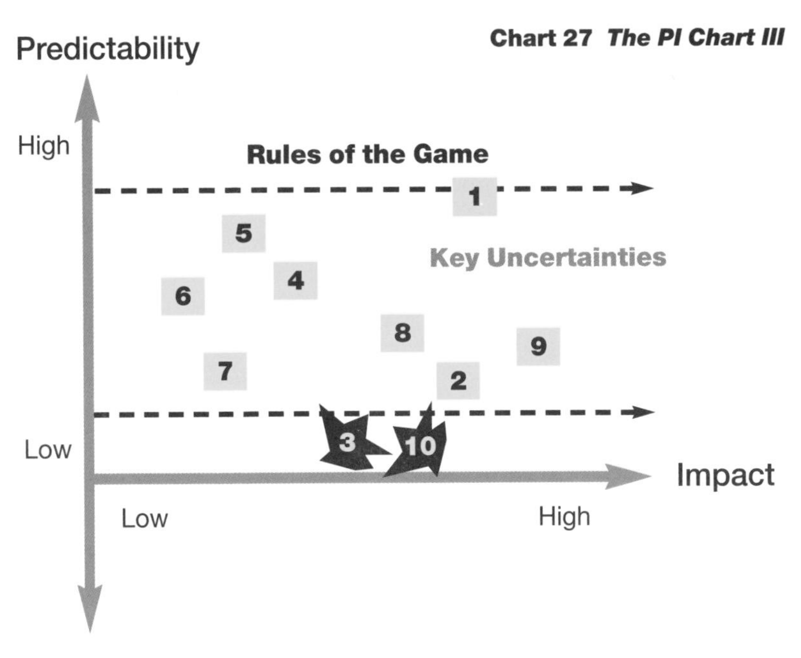

to mind. All you can do is work out what the sensitivity of your profit and loss account is to each of these factors and what you will do if they change direction. Some guru was once asked how he knew when a trend was no longer a trend. His response: when it becomes a turning point! Foxes shrug their shoulders and get on with life.

We'd like to back up this chart with some practical examples. Let's start with a farmer. Weather is a key uncertainty. It's completely out of his control so what can he do about it? He could shoot rain-making rockets into the sky, which is what some governments do, but he probably hasn't got the resources to do that. Apart from which, if he is successful, he runs the risk of incurring the ire of other farmers in the neighbourhood who will think he's swiped their rain. Seriously, though, his options appear to be as follows. He can consult meteorologists as the year progresses to improve his intelligence on whether the season is going to be a good one weather-wise or not. He can watch TV weather forecasts. He can make a strategic decision to sell his farm and buy one on the other side of the mountain where it's known to rain more frequently. He can put in an irrigation system to take the variability of rainfall almost out of play. He can switch crops or animals to ones which are more naturally accustomed to dry conditions. Or he can get out of the farming business altogether and turn his farm into bed-and-breakfast accommodation. Alternatively, if he has the money and the acreage, he can consider turning it into a game farm.

Another example would be a business that is a national champion in a dodgy country where politics is a key uncertainty. The obvious strategy would be to expand the geographical footprint of the business to reduce dependence on the future of that one country. Perhaps a key uncertainty surrounds the future demand for a product, in which case diversification of the company's portfolio of products would be wise. In both cases, the scope of the company would be revisited. On the other hand, maybe a competitor has a strategy or technology up its sleeve, which is a key uncertainty. In this event, should the company form an alliance with the competitor or take it over? If your operations are energy-intensive and the oil price is a key uncertainty, how will you reconfigure the design of your plant to cut back on energy consumption in the production process?

All these examples have a common theme. Identify the uncertainty and do some form of risk assessment in terms of severity of impact and probability of occurrence. You then have different options in terms of managing the risk. Reduce it by reducing its probability (the frequency of road accidents is diminished by driving slower). Reduce it by mitigating its impact (the impact is mitigated by buying a car with airbags as well as by wearing a seatbelt and driving slower). Eliminate it (by stopping driving altogether and moving into an old-age home). Transfer the risk with insurance. Or retain the risk and live with it. You can flaunt your two-carat flawless white diamond and insure it; or put it in a safe and wear a zircon replica (like some Hollywood movie stars do, knowing they have the original back home); or if you're really conservative do both (insure it and wear the replica). It's up to you, and collectively it's up to the company, once the risk has been identified.

Our PI Chart can also be adjusted to identify trends that have developed over time, or how a key uncertainty's degree of predictability and impact has changed. An excellent example is how HIV / AIDS has evolved through different stages of predictability and impact in sub-Saharan Africa compared to most Western countries (see diagram overleaf).

From its beginnings as an unknown unknown in 1980, through its status as a wild card and key uncertainty in the 1980s and 1990s, HIV / AIDS is now a rule of the game with an

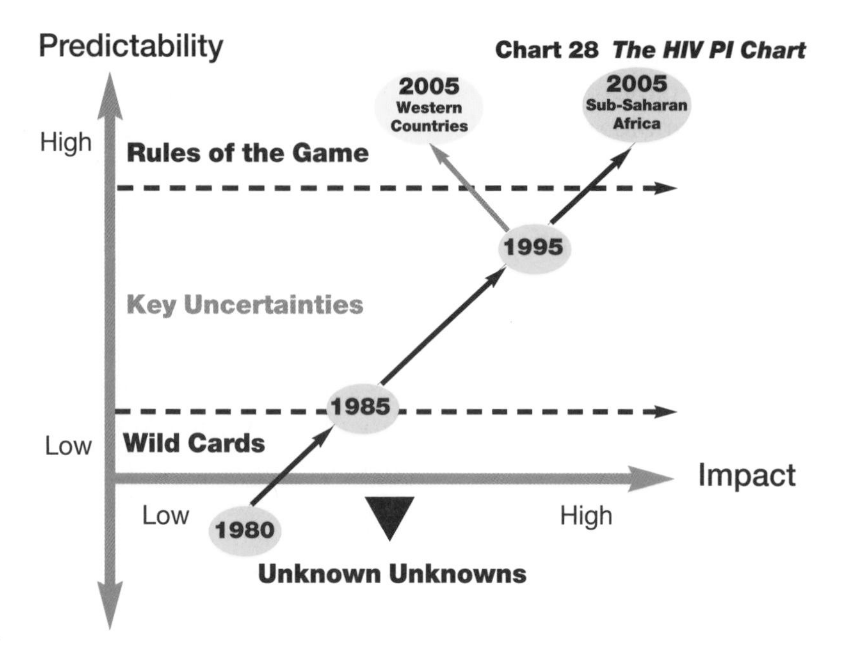

impact which is anticipated to be lower in Western countries than in sub-Saharan Africa. However, it remains a key uncertainty in China and India.

We'll end off this section with a quote from a well-known children's song: "If you go down to the woods today, you're in for a big surprise." Traditionally, woods were not places to venture. Danger in the guise of a big bad wolf lurked therein, ready to pounce on an unwary traveller. Of course, in the case of the song, the surprise was nothing worse than a teddy bear's picnic. Companies sometimes end up in the woods and then two proverbs spring to mind: "Can't see the wood for the trees" (can't see the big picture) and "You're not out of the woods yet" (you're still in a tricky situation).

In both proverbs, 'woods' are places of confusion and difficulty, a somewhat intimidating and irregular clump of trees. We have found that this part of the conversation more than any other turns executives into foxes. They see the big picture and therefore know how to plot grand strategies. They see the small picture and let no fine detail escape them. In short, they see the woods *and* the trees and are well prepared for surprises. With these capabilities, they can be out of the woods in a flash – with only fox prints to show they were ever there.

Scenarios

I skate to where the puck is going to be,
not to where it has been.
WAYNE GRETZKY

We all love a good story. Whether it's in a book we are reading or movie we are watching, we are drawn in by the richness of the characters, the excitement of the plot, the beauty of the locations, and we have a fascination with how the story will pan out. We continually work through possible outcomes and test these against the events as they unfold, taking pleasure when we get things right and enjoying the surprise when we don't. Our love of stories is generally initiated when we are young. Stories told with relish by parents and teachers have the effect of not only entertaining young minds, but also of exercising them. They are also used to convey messages and lessons in life's morals and virtues, the most common being that good always wins over evil – ugly stepsisters don't get handsome princes!

Storytelling is an important part of all cultures. Africa, especially, is blessed with stories passed down over hundreds of years that are as applicable now as they were when they were first told. At an early age, children in Botswana are taught the story of the wolf and the fox that found a small hole in a fence surrounding a farmer's chicken coop. The two squeezed through and celebrated their find by feasting on the hapless chickens. Whereas the fox made a point of interrupting his feeding, returning periodically to the hole in the fence, the wolf took advantage of the windfall to gorge himself. When they heard the farmer coming with his gun the two rushed back to the hole to escape. The fox, who had kept checking to see that he could still fit, slipped through the hole effortlessly. The wolf however, now full and fat, got stuck and paid the ultimate price.

But the value of stories doesn't end when we leave childhood behind us. They are found wherever there is creative thought. Purely analytical thought, on the other hand, demands the comforting discipline of parameters – hence the popularity of accounting among those who don't want to become actuaries! Analytical thinking therefore runs the risk of ignoring factors outside of its parameters; and this is the main reason why, in an environment of growing uncertainty, traditional forms of analytical strategising are inappropriate. What is needed is open-ended thought and imagination that spirals around possibilities and scenarios – the type of mental process used by Detectives Sturgis, Rebus and Banks in solving the murder mysteries created by their originators, Jonathan Kellerman, Ian Rankin and Peter Robinson. Even Agatha Christie's Hercule Poirot – the doyen of detectives – played scenarios which at first seemed outrageous and implausible until all was revealed.

Scenarios are particularly useful in modern strategy for a number of reasons. Firstly, they have the capacity to change minds in a non-prescriptive manner. If people are encouraged to imagine a possible scenario that is better than the one they're in at the moment, they are able to imagine the positive consequences of operating in such a scenario. This allows them to develop an enthusiasm for the task at hand and helps them change of their own volition. Much better than order-

Chart 29 ***The Conversation Model – Scenarios***

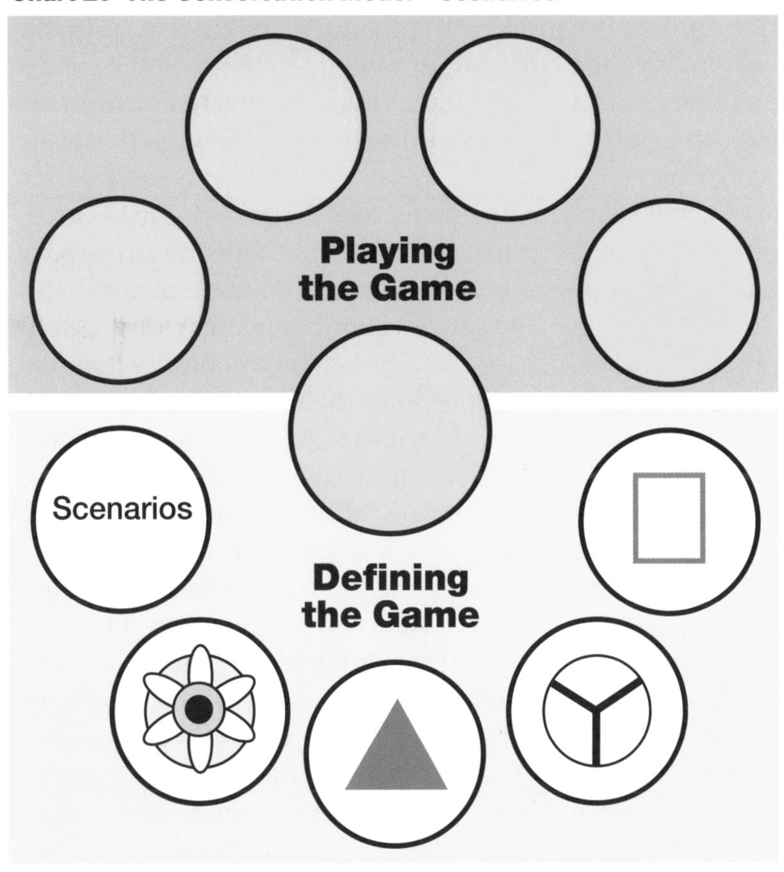

ing them around or forcing them to change. Similarly, the use of scenarios in strategy builds a collective alignment amongst the teams using them, thereby enhancing efficiencies and creating a renewed sense of purpose to fulfil whatever strategic or tactical decisions are made. People often find it easier to comprehend information if it is in the form of a scenario rather than a list of facts and figures. For this reason, scenarios provide a clearer understanding of the complexities of any game. Trying to understand, say, a referee's rulebook is easier if you can imagine a situation unfolding in the game to which the rule applies. But unlike the certainty of the rules of sport, the rules of business are fraught with uncertainty and parameters that can change in a blur. The most effective way, therefore, to make sense of this uncertainty is through the use of scenarios.

So where can you buy scenarios? There seems to be an expectation that there are scenarios 'out there' for any type of business and one only has to, say, find the correct website, download the relevant set of scenarios and plan accordingly; or call in a set of scenario specialists who will flex their minds, ask some challenging questions, digest the data and feed it back in a neat package of scenarios. Conventional scenario planning indeed relies on teams of such specialists who draw up elegant and intricate stories about the future. After due consultation and iteration, these are then offered to the client as a range of possible outcomes. However, they are generally 'big' pictures – long but well-written scenarios – that have been developed by specialists and not by the decision-makers themselves. For business leaders, some of whom have an attention span shorter than a TV ad, it makes for a somewhat laborious read; but the generality of the scenarios can also have the effect of diluting their relevance for operations management in the company, thereby reducing their buy-in.

No self-respecting businessman is willing to risk spending money on something over which he has no influence. Influence is leverage; influence is power. It is the difference between success through strategy and success through luck. If business is a game, players win because they are *active* participants, not *passive* receptors; and this is the point of differentiation between our model and traditional forms of scenario planning methodology.

If scenarios are to be relevant and effective, it would seem logical that they should be prepared by the people who feature in them, and they should incorporate an element over which those same people have a degree of influence. In other words, based on our terms of reference, the most relevant scenarios in the game of business are those prepared *by* the players, *for* the players and *featuring* the players themselves as stars *in* the game. This inclusive philosophy is the essence of our book. We believe in a form of strategic thinking which recognises the complexity of the games we are in and yet provides us with the most effective way to *play* the game. The purpose of scenarios is therefore to create a better future, to win the game. We're talking proactive stuff, not just responding to futures completely outside our control.

This is one of the reasons we avoid using the phrase 'driving forces', which is much in vogue among scenario planners. It implies that you're not the driver. As John Connor said in *The Terminator*: "The future isn't set. The only fate is what we make for ourselves." Bearing this in mind, the core of our approach can be represented in the following diagram:

Chart 30 ***The Scenario Gameboard I***

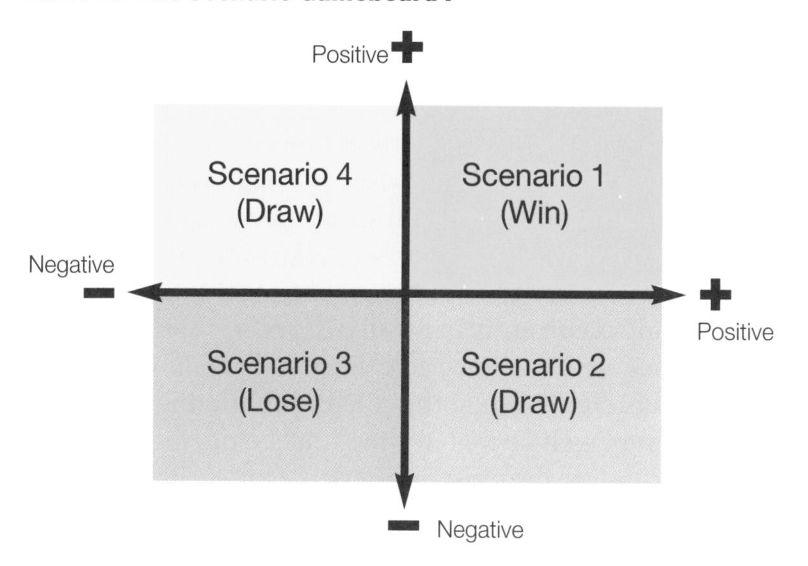

We have called it the Scenario Gameboard. Like any other gameboard, it represents an interactive game with more than one player. That's what business essentially is, unless you're a monopoly. The movement of a particular player, or several players, can be 'plotted' on the board. There is an ugly corner of the gameboard that should be avoided (scenario 3 in our diagram) and there is a sunny corner that offers all sorts of benefits should you land there (scenario 1). There are also parts of the gameboard with mixed fortunes (scenario 2 and scenario 4).

Consequently, your success can be judged by your movement and position on the gameboard. As with most other games, there are events out of the control of the players, like the outcome of the throw of the dice, and yet there are definite advantages to knowing how to play the game better than the other players. You have a better chance of winning, and that is the intent of business.

We often like to imagine the scenarios represented on a gameboard as if they were neighbouring countries on a map. In the description of the scenarios, we include some markers or flags by which you can recognise the current position on the gameboard the company occupies. We then delineate future paths across the board that a company can take, depending on how the external environment changes, how the company responds, or a bit of both. The flags and shift in language will announce when the company is crossing the borders into a new country (or scenario). The purpose obviously is to avoid paths that descend into negative territory if the company is currently in positive territory; and if it is currently in negative territory, to choose paths that will lead it out and avoid paths (like the plague) that will lead it further in. It may well be that, for the time being, the company will not move into the most desirable scenario, either because current circumstances don't permit it or the company has to pass through another scenario on the journey there (direct access being barred).

There are ways though in which the concept of our scenario gameboard differs from the common idea of a gameboard. The most significant is that there is no set gameboard. It is not designed by any third party and bought across the counter in a toyshop. The very people playing the game design it. The players therefore don't have to try and read through the rules, because they know the rules of the game. They are therefore best qualified to play the game. Wouldn't it be great if we could design a game so that we would always win? We would write the rules to our advantage and skew the conditions so that we commanded the most leverage.

But the game of business is not like that. As we know, most events that shape the game are outside of our control and many of them are uncertain; and we also don't make all the rules ourselves. A new rule, for instance, creeping into Formula One racing and Premier League soccer is that money determines the winners. This makes the winner more predictable and the sport more boring to watch. Loss of audience is a distinct possibility so the resultant gameboard has to reflect that – a mixture of good and bad scenarios. If we are to achieve any form of control over our future by playing the game better than others, then the identification of the pivotal uncertainties shaping these scenarios is critical.

So, how is this possible? The answer lies in the midst of the PI Chart (*Chart 27*) we presented in the last section. It is amongst the key uncertainties listed there as conceivably having the most impact on the company that the ones most relevant to the development of the scenarios will be found. Their selection is a cause for conversation, intuition and prudent facilitation.

If a company has been open and honest in its strategic conversation, the PI Chart should consist of a small collection of the most important key uncertainties. If the PI Chart is congested, it is for one of two reasons: either the uncertainties haven't been winnowed down properly, or the company is in a minefield of uncertainties and should call in a helicopter to be airlifted! Invariably though, closer examination of, and conversation around, these key uncertainties will identify similarities between two or more of them. This will make it easier to cluster them, because scenarios should never be too narrowly defined. If the key uncertainties are too specific, the scenarios they produce can quickly become redundant and so does the gameboard. Similarly, using key uncertainties that are too broad produces vast and fuzzy scenarios in which it is difficult to position yourself. Examples of effective clustering would put commodity prices, exchange rates and physical demand for your product under the label 'market'; while unit costs of production, output per man hour and other productivity parameters would be merged under the heading 'efficiency'. The breadth of the scenarios will also depend on their required time frame – the longer the time frame the broader the scenarios ought to be. It is also quite possible to sweep up some of the remaining uncertainties into the text of the scenarios, even if they are not used in determining the axes of the gameboard. Obviously the logic of the scenarios must be able to accommodate the additions made.

We have found that sometimes when a company is able to see the most relevant key uncertainties plotted on its PI Chart, there will be little disagreement as to which uncertainties will act as axes for the scenario matrix, because they will be quite obvious. Generally, though, further conversation should take place around possible candidates, with intuition being the deciding factor; after all, those playing the game every day tend to have a sixth sense about the twists and turns that should be part and parcel of the gameboard.

To nudge consensus along on the identification of the

scenario drivers, sensible facilitation is required. We don't like to be prescriptive, but here are some guidelines:

1. Using two key uncertainties that are outside of a company's control will produce four scenarios in which, at best, the company can adapt its strategy or be more resourceful. Traditional scenarios are generally composed of uncertainties of this type. There is nothing wrong with this if two variables in the external environment stand out so sharply that they cannot be ignored. But things can fall a bit flat. As we've already emphasised, a gameboard that confers some control to the players themselves as to where they end up on the board is likely to get a more positive reception.
2. Using two key uncertainties that are within a company's control or influence will produce four scenarios that are applicable if the company is concerned with a more internal focus, such as a change in management style. For example, one company used the presence and absence of people-centred policies on one axis and output-oriented policies on the other.
3. Using one key uncertainty that is outside of the company's control and one that is within the company's control will produce four scenarios where the company has a measure of influence over its destiny. At the very least, it will be prepared for changes in the external environment. We find this combination the most empowering in that it recognises both sides of the equation.

Purists may complain that we're stretching the definition of scenario planning too far by allowing the principal actor (the company) to play such a prominent role in the way the scenarios unfold. Scenarios should only depict external developments, they may argue; and aren't you contradicting the principle that scenarios should be beyond the control of the company to which they apply? However, our experience has shown us that the enthusiasm and imagination displayed by people in formulating scenarios is directly related to how much they participate in the story line. Everyone wants a part! So you have to imagine that a scenario is like a Greek tragedy where free will is a delusion and the Fates decide your destiny. Indeed, Delphi may claim to be the source of scenario planning. The oracle there was so outrageously ambiguous that its utterances covered all eventualities. Purveyors of omens and scenarios have a lot in common!

We are sometimes asked during a facilitation whether more than two pivotal uncertainties can be used to design a scenario gameboard. It may be the case that, say, three key uncertainties seem to be equally important in defining a company's possible future. In such a situation the scenario gameboard would comprise eight different scenarios, as follows:

Chart 31 ***The Scenario Gameboard II***

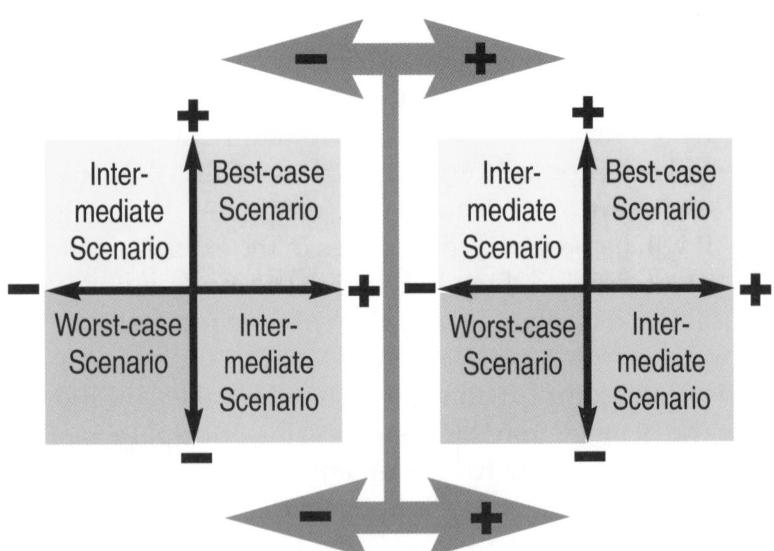

What a nightmare! By the time you get to the seventh scenario, someone is bound to ask what the real difference is between that one and the second one – by which time you'll have forgotten what the second one is!

One company actually wanted a cube made of wire so that the three dimensions could be more obviously expressed. An octet of scenarios would have hung inside the cube. Luckily we dissuaded them from this venture before construction began. The only justification for doing something as complicated as this would be if the variable on each side of the vertical line was within the company's control, while the matrices on each side were determined by a pair of external variables beyond the company's control. You might, say, have four global scenarios against which you want to compare a focused strategy with a diversified one to see which is more robust. Even then, it may be stretching the mind too far to go into eight dimensions.

Returning to earth, the objective of using the scenario gameboard is to make sense of the future, not to increase its complexity beyond our ability to respond. For this reason we recommend a gameboard with a minimum of two and a maximum of four scenarios. Remember that the radar screen has already captured the uncertainties, so they are not lost; and by monitoring the radar screen it is possible to see if a key uncertainty moves up the ranking and needs further analysis in the scenario formulation phase.

But the purpose of our process is not simply to attain a product (the scenarios); and it must be emphasised that there is no right or wrong set of scenarios. The value of the process lies in its power to create an awareness of the game that would normally remain hidden in conventional forms of developing strategy. That is why we have opted for a range of two to four scenarios. It may just be that two scenarios work to transform thinking. It did in South Africa with the *High Road* of negotiation leading to a political settlement; and the *Low Road* of confrontation leading to civil war and a wasteland. If the gameboard had been around in 1986 when these scenarios were launched, it would have been divided into two halves, the left being the *High Road* and the right being the *Low Road*. In business, two scenarios can also do the job, where one is the official future generated by consensus thinking (sometimes called *Conventional Wisdom*) and the other is a surprising future generated by the imagination. Nevertheless, we prefer a 2 x 2 matrix. It's a lens through which people are accustomed to look at the future. Once the scenario drivers have been identified, they are expressed as intersecting variable axes to produce four possible scenarios: one a worst-case scenario (you lose the game), one a best-case scenario (victory) and the other two intermediate scenarios (drawn games). *Chart 32* opposite illustrates this. Where the negative version of one variable overrides the positive version of the other variable, the scenario may be logically impossible. In that event, a cross will appear in that quadrant, ruling it out and bringing the total number of scenarios down to three.

It is important to have both positive and negative scenarios on the gameboard, because often as much strategic insight is gained from avoiding or surviving a negative scenario as is obtained from taking advantage of a positive one. A classic example of the educational value of a negative scenario was provided at a workshop on the future of a church hemmed in by business parks in the centre of Johannesburg. The exodus of residents from the suburb had caused the congregation to decline in numbers and to raise its average age. A young lady was asked to write a negative scenario and she came up with a real beauty. It was called *Geriatric Swansong*. In the scenario, the congregation gradually died off until there was only one member left. He came to church on Sundays to take communion; so did the vicar, the choir, the

Chart 32 ***The Scenario Gameboard III***

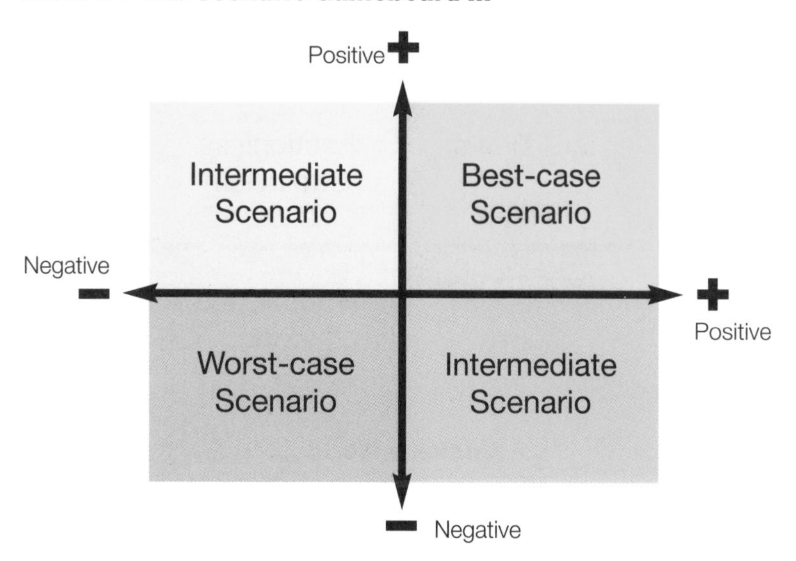

choir mistress and the organist. Then he died and the church was turned into a nightclub called 'The Club of Joy' and it was not ecclesiastical joy that was being dished out in the club. Anyway, this scenario was distributed in the parish newsletter, evoking a strong reaction about how the church should be stopped from being turned into a nightclub. It had far more motivational effect than the positive scenario, which was rather boringly called *Onward Christian Soldiers*.

In a number of our facilitations, we have found that multinational companies like to work with positive and negative global scenarios. One of the key uncertainties surrounds the global market, which is identified in the horizontal 'x' axis as a strong versus a weak market. The other uncertainty concerns the political state of the world, and is expressed on the vertical 'y' axis as a stable versus unstable world. The four possible scenarios that emerge in the matrix (going clockwise from the top right) are shown in *Chart 33* on the following page.

Chart 33 ***The Multinational Gameboard***

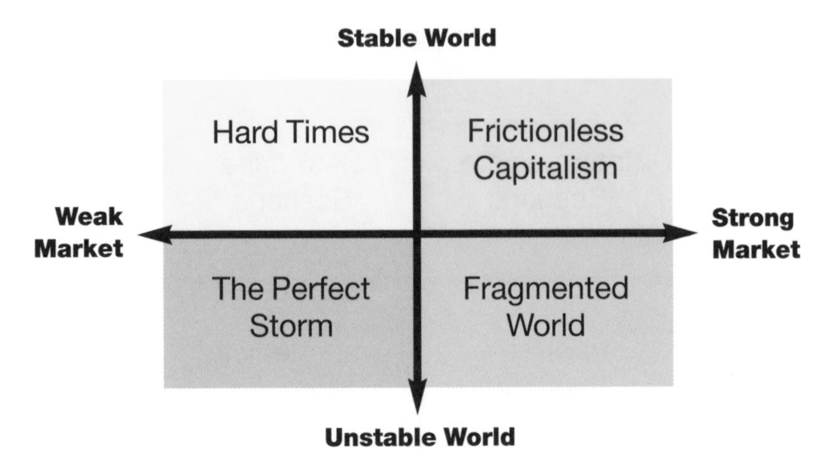

1 Frictionless Capitalism

This is the best scenario, being a strong market in a stable world where globalisation continues. It's very much business as usual, the only difference being that the global economy becomes more 'multipolar' with the rise of Chindia (China and India). The company's geographical footprint has to be re-examined in this light.

2 Fragmented World

This is a mixed scenario where markets remain strong despite a world of increasing animosity and 'no go' areas for multinationals. The profit potential in some countries diminishes as a result of new taxes, royalties and regulations being enacted by governments whose outlook is increasingly nationalistic. Consequently, investment strategies have to become more selective.

3 The Perfect Storm

This is the worst scenario where terrorism and regional strife chuck so much sand in the wheels of frictionless capitalism that the world economy dives into full-scale recession. Security of supply lines for key commodities such as oil become paramount. All company hatches have to be battened down to survive the storm.

4 Hard Times

This is a scenario of a normal economic downturn caused by the usual suspects of governments and consumers overextending themselves and building up an inordinate amount of debt, stock markets getting too greedy, companies installing too much extra production capacity, etc. Eventually the cycle reverses when everyone has learnt the lesson (temporarily). Maintaining a positive cash flow during the downturn is vital, so that the company emerges stronger than its competitors when it is over.

The question is: which scenario are we in at the moment and where will we be next year? You choose. Multinational companies can also use this matrix to plot the direction of the individual countries in which they own businesses or to which they sell their products. For instance, a country with a stable sociopolitical structure and a growing free-market economy can be assigned to *Frictionless Capitalism*. On the other hand, a country with a stable sociopolitical structure but a weak economy can be located in *Hard Times*, and so on. The gameboard thereby recognises that there is no overall strategy that can be considered optimal for a multinational. Instead, the company's scenario gameboard should be rolled down to the operating unit in each country with the conversation at that level focusing on how best to move forward in that particular market. Such an approach respects the complexity of a multinational's sphere of operations.

An alternative way of assessing individual countries and

their respective markets in terms of sociopolitical stability and the competitiveness of their markets puts them all on the same gameboard. It goes like this:

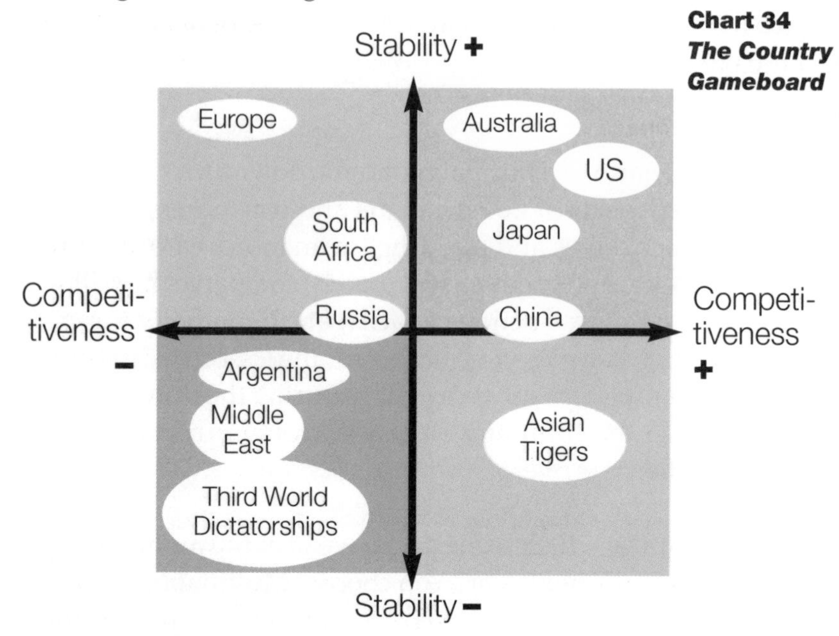

Chart 34
The Country Gameboard

You might disagree with some of the locations we've given to countries. But that's the whole point of the gameboard: to excite debate.

Now let's examine a company typically operating within a *national* market. The 'x' axis of the gameboard signifies the state of the market in which the company is selling its goods and services (beyond its control), and the 'y' axis the efficiency of the company (within its control). As we've already remarked, you have to unpack the yardsticks by which you judge whether the market is positive or negative and your efficiency is rising or falling. Another point you have to decide on is whether you express your change in efficiency in absolute or relative terms, i.e. whether you exclude or include the performance of your chief competitors in making the judgement as to whether your efficiency has improved or declined. That you should take into account the performance of your competitors is unquestionable. But there are two alternatives: you can make the 'y' axis represent relative efficiency or, as you will see shortly, you can plot your competitors' progress on the same gameboard.

Here's the most popular gameboard in our experience of facilitation:

Chart 35
The Business Gameboard I

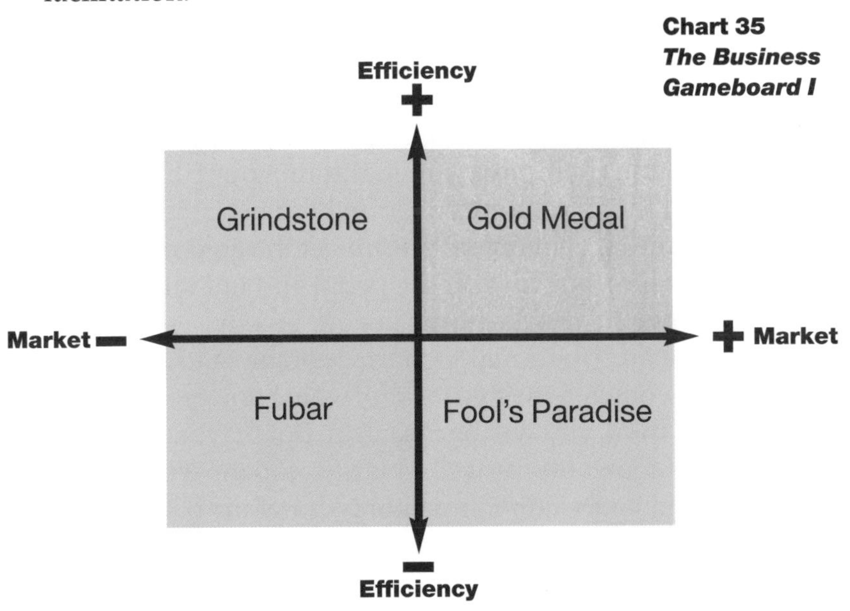

We are pretty confident that when examining this diagram, you can immediately project an image of each scenario in your mind without having to stop and analyse it. How's this possible? The names. For those readers who are not veterans of the war in Vietnam, the mystery of *Fubar* will be resolved in the next paragraph.

Obviously, the worst-case scenario is where your competitiveness is declining in a poor market. A strategist with a sense of humour called this scenario *Fubar* during the actual conversation. Afterwards, she bailed out in the written version and renamed it *Mubar – mucked up beyond any recognition*. But *Fubar* is now well established in the oral tradition of the company. Nobody wants to be in it because it is the last stage before bankruptcy and death. The second scenario of *Fool's Paradise* is where all your faults are covered up by a booming market. Should the market turn and you do nothing you go straight into the *Fubar*.

The third scenario, *Grindstone*, is where you put your nose to the grindstone and grind out better efficiencies than your competitors in a hostile market. We've all been there! And the final scenario is aptly named *Gold Medal* because, like any great Olympic champion, you maintain your competitive streak into the *next* games despite being showered with success in the current ones. You still get the gold medal. It's so easy to take your foot off the pedal and fall into a *Fool's Paradise* when the market turns in your favour.

As in the multinational scenario, you have to ask yourself where you were five years ago, where you are now and where you think you will be next year. But maybe you want to include a competitor as well. You're Company A in the next diagram and your main competitor is Company B. Company B is a large company that has been in the market longer than you have and historically has been very successful in holding on to its client base. You have had issues with efficiency which up till now a blinkered management structure has ignored. Examined against the backdrop of the gameboard, you have been residing in a *Fool's Paradise*. Your competitor, by contrast, has regularly been winning gold medals. However, buoyed by the positive market, Company B is beginning to show complacency, whereas you recognise that you are trailing in the game because of your relative inefficiency and are aware that, if the market worsens, you will be *Fubarred*. You start putting measures in place to address this. Because of factors outside of the control of both companies, the market does indeed worsen. You, having worked through the strategy for change, are prepared, and move into the *Grindstone* scenario. Company B is unprepared for the deterioration in market conditions and overnight sees its dominance in the market disappear. Why? Because you've seized its market share. You are now in a perfect position to make a takeover bid for company B (which you could never have done on the other side of the gameboard because everything is expensive when market conditions are good).

Chart 36
The Business Gameboard II

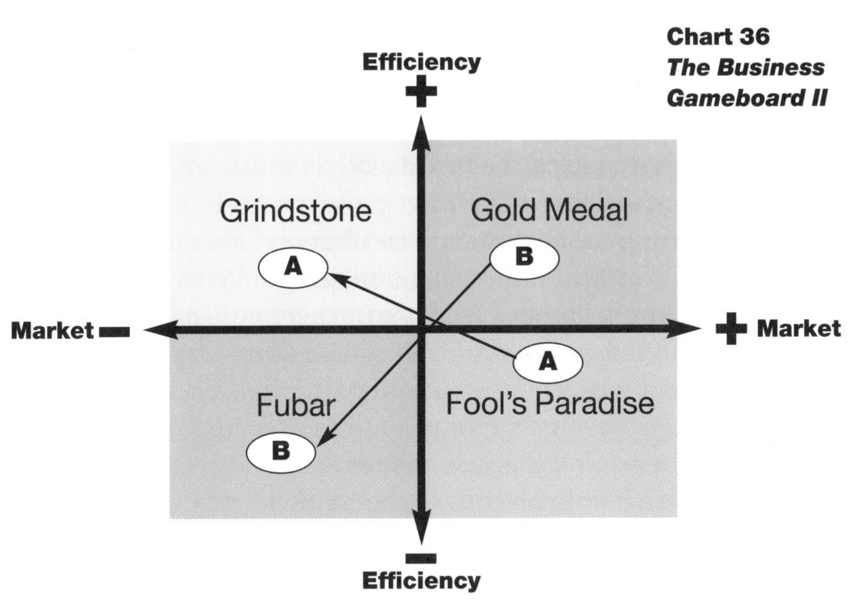

The names of the scenarios are a fundamental part of their character as well as their marketability. One of the biggest selling range of toys in the UK is called *Bob the Builder*, based on the TV show which features stories around the character and his team made up of Roley the roller, Scoop the excavator, Dizzy the cement mixer, Lofty the crane and Travis the tractor. Young children crave miniature replicas of earth-moving machinery and tractors as long as they go under these brand names. You hear infants cry out for *Bob the Boodah* and *Bob the Biddah*. In the old days, we had Meccano with iron struts with little holes in them that could be bolted together. Then came *Lego*, which is still popular. Now to satisfy the urge to be in the construction game, we have *Bob the Builder*. It's all in the name! The difference is that Bob teaches children about teamwork, whereas the other games are mainly solo efforts.

But there is value in a scenario name beyond the image it creates in the minds of those involved in the process. The best-case scenario, if summed up in a short, punchy title, can be used to communicate a change in the direction of the company to all employees and get them emotionally involved. Names fit on tags and flashcards, buttonholes and post-its. Even bumper stickers can be employed to get the message across. Finding the correct name is often a challenge, as it invariably sparks heated conversation around the merit of one name over another (especially if an ad agency is hauled in as well). But in the end the process can be quite inspiring and fun. Here's a hint, though: avoid using *Heaven* as a name for a best-case scenario. It may sound ideal but you have to die to get there! *Utopia* is just as bad.

Yet, while a name can convey the character of a scenario, it can't always create the exact meaning for the company in the context of the game. After all, different people attach different meanings to the same word. Take *Chihuahua*. People who have a fear of dogs will immediately feel an aversion to the word because they will picture being 'chowed' in the street by one of them. They're good at scampering back and forth under gates and doing the savaging in between. Yet dog lovers would consider such a dog hanging on to their trouser leg as nothing more than a nuisance (unless it leaves bite marks in the trousers). For this reason, each scenario needs to be clarified and explained further than just giving it a name. Conventional scenario planning demands rich and expansive stories. Our experience is that, however noble their intention, such stories are often impractical, tedious and unread. Whatever form scenarios take, they should be depicted in a concise and logical way – as in an executive summary. Language should be home-brewed, picking up on the everyday 'lingo' used by operating management. Fancy prose bombs out. Information to develop the scenarios should come from those expected to keep an eye on future developments pertaining to their scope of operations. A representative from the human resources department would provide input, say, on impending labour regulations; similarly a representative from the procurement office would contribute his piece on the security of raw material supplies. It is important to include a cross section of perspectives in the scenarios in order to make people think out of their silos.

A great example of getting different parts of a company to cross-fertilise their ideas through scenarios concerns energy. Here is a commodity which everybody uses and which has recently seen a jump in its price, whether you're talking oil, coal or electricity. We've chosen the uncertainty about the validity of global warming and the greenhouse effect as one axis, and the level of the oil price as the other axis. Our gameboard to get the creative juices flowing therefore looks something like *Chart 37* on the next page.

Doing the clockwise routine from top right, we have the following scenarios:

Gasoline Alley

After the recent spike, oil prices resume the low level at which they've been for most of the last 140 years (ever since the Pennsylvanian oil fields were discovered). New oil reserves

Chart 37 ***The Energy Gameboard***

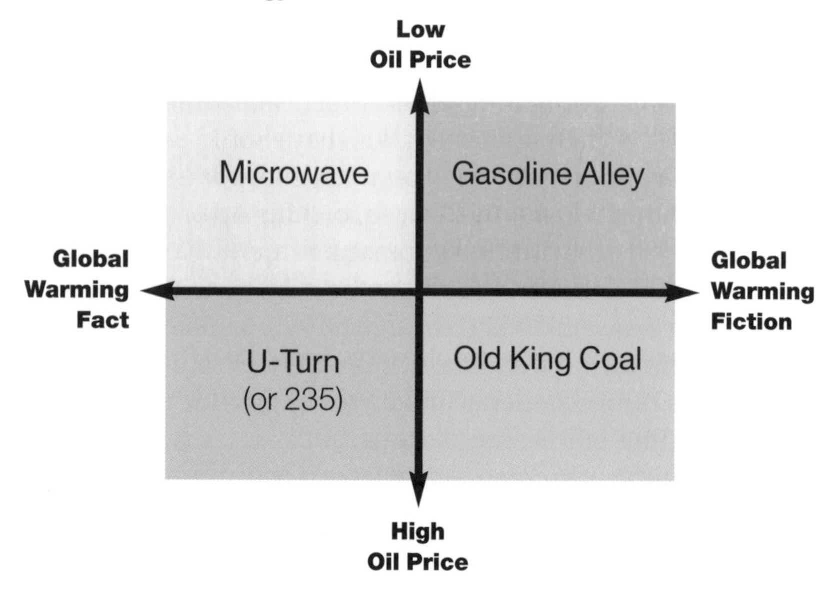

are found to satisfy the growing appetite of the world's most populous countries like China, India and Brazil. With all the extra carbon dioxide emissions, the world's climate shows no ostensible change. People therefore assume that global warming was a myth.

Old King Coal

Increased instability in the Middle East, a jittery OPEC and lack of new oil discoveries to keep up with demand push the price of oil into the stratosphere at around $100 a barrel. This is particularly worrying for heavy industry, which immediately puts in place enormous energy-saving drives. Solar power, wind power, tidal power and hydropower cannot be made energy-intensive enough to be a viable alternative on a large scale. The best answer seems to be coal, because the world still has vast reserves to be mined. Modern and very efficient coal-burning power stations replace oil-burning stations, and

SASOL's oil-from-coal processing methodology is given a significant boost. People meanwhile turn to hybrid cars (petrol / electric) and fuel-cell cars in greater numbers. They stop driving SUVs to the office or to drop their kids at school. At $100 a barrel you 'invest' in your petrol tank and decide very carefully on the portfolio of activities on which it is to be consumed!

U-Turn or 235 (representing enriched uranium)

Combined with a growing shortage of oil, global warming detection systems reveal a noticeable increase in the planet's average temperature. International limitations on carbon emissions come into immediate effect. A switch to coal is therefore ruled out. As a result, there is a significant injection of new capital into research for alternative energy systems. However, none of these can satisfy the base load of power demand from industry, and so countries around the globe re-examine the merits of nuclear energy. This 'U-Turn' gains momentum as new and safer techniques of handling nuclear energy and disposing of waste are invented. However, with more uranium being transported between mines, enrichment plants and power stations, the threat of terrorists gaining access to fissionable material for nuclear weapons rises.

Microwave

Low oil prices and continuing controversy over global warming mean no change in energy consumption patterns. But the 'doomsayers' are right and the world's temperature inexorably goes up by a few degrees over the next fifty years. The consequences are huge, as sea levels rise and low-lying areas are permanently flooded. Local climate change speaks disaster for farmers.

These descriptions paint a brief picture of the suite of scenarios, and allude to their different characteristics. As the output of a proper scenario session, each description would be, say, about a page and a half to two pages in length; or, alternatively, it could be expressed in a series of bullet points on the gameboard itself.

Identifying the differences between the scenarios is an important part of the process. Just as meteorologists are able to recognise signs of developing thunder activity, contributors to a strategic conversation that define the scenarios should also draw up a list of 'red flags' that might herald the onset of a certain scenario. These may include signs of political instability in a country that provides a company's raw materials; 'chatter' around possible import/export regulations; new technological developments that may shift the balance of power in an industry; and legal precedents that induce consumers to lead a more healthy lifestyle. The 'red flag' process should be highly inclusive and rolled down throughout the company *after* the strategic direction of a company and its preferred scenario have been communicated to staff. In their strategic conversations, staff can be encouraged to put forward their own 'red flags' for evaluation.

On a different note, we'd like to outline a scenario gameboard we recently designed for the City of Cape Town and presented at a banquet there. It contains the following pivotal uncertainties:

1. The inclusivity/exclusivity of the local economy. An inclusive economy would be one that links the mainstream economy in Cape Town itself to all the informal economies that are sprouting up in disadvantaged areas around the city.
2. Sustainable/unsustainable development. This focuses on the relationship between the future development of the city and its natural and physical environment (re-

membering that the Western Cape is one of the richest floral kingdoms in the world).

The gameboard for Cape Town therefore looked like this:

Chart 38 *The City Gameboard*

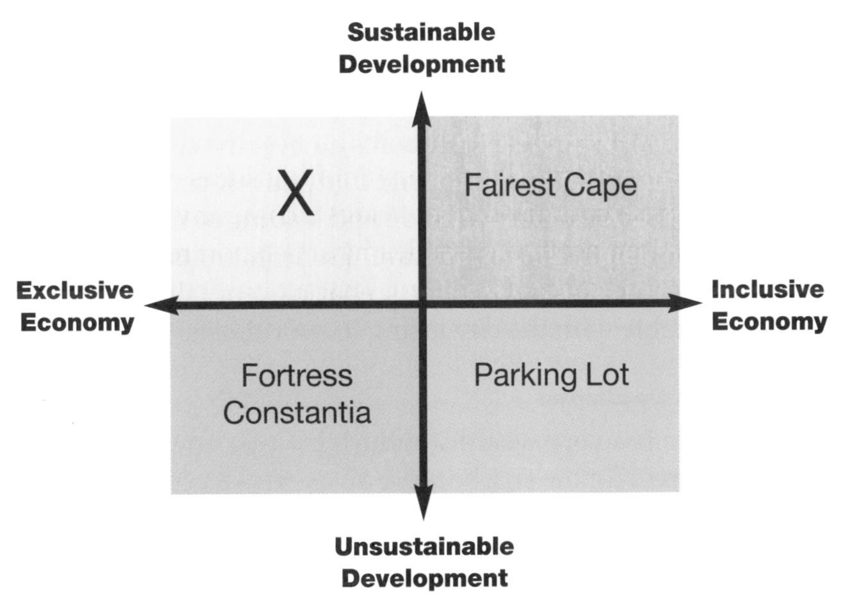

Because it is not possible from a humanitarian point of view to achieve sustainable development in an exclusive economy, there are only three possible scenarios:

Fairest Cape

This is the best-case scenario. Everything clicks together. Big business starts to partner with small business through procurement contracts and other means. An enormous drive to assist entrepreneurs throughout the region to establish businesses and gain access to capital is put in place. Environmental sensitivities are respected, thereby ensuring that the city retains its appeal as a unique tourist destination. The Cape is fairest in beauty and fairest in offering everybody a better life for all.

Parking Lot

This name is derived from a line in the Joni Mitchell song *Big Yellow Taxi:* "They paved paradise and put up a parking lot."

As the name suggests, property developers have a field day and small business mushrooms all over the city in an uncontrolled way. In time, informal trade envelops the streets, usurping the role of formal trade and leading to the physical degradation of the infrastructure. Environmental concerns escalate, water runs out and the scenario eventually becomes unsustainable with the city losing its world-class status.

Fortress Constantia

Constantia is a very wealthy suburb in Cape Town. It turns into a fortress for the rich because an exclusive economy creates few jobs in the poorer areas. Informal trading is suppressed and unemployment increases, contributing to a soaring crime rate. Residential developments take the form of cluster housing projects with high walls and plenty of security guards. However, movement becomes so restricted that getting to and from Cape Town International airport becomes a mission. Tourism fades and there's no money in the coffers to keep the environment in good order.

To summarise, the gameboard should consist of three or four scenarios that have emerged from the pivotal uncertainties; each scenario should have an original name that evokes the character of that scenario in the mind of the reader; and attached to each scenario should be a rich yet concise narrative drawn from the experience of the different actors in the organisation concerned. Is there anything else? Well, you've had a taste of the various gameboards. We think, in addition, it's a good thing to position your organisation on the gameboard according to where you've come from and where you are now, given current realities. Then you have to project where you want to be next year and in, say, five years' time. The path may be hard to follow and events outside of your control may make it impossible. You may also wish to position your competitors and gauge your outlook relative to theirs. Above all, the secret to playing the game lies in the question: *what if?* What if a certain scenario starts to materialise and we want to move towards or away from it? What if a competitor moves towards the best-case scenario ahead of us? What if we could turn the game to our advantage? What if we do nothing? The answers to these questions lie in a judicious appraisal of the company's strengths, weaknesses, opportunities and threats for each of the scenarios. That's right. *Now* it's time to do a SWOT analysis.

SWOT

It is a sublime thing to suffer and be stronger.

HENRY WADSWORTH LONGFELLOW

At this stage, we move from defining the game to playing the game. The conversation should as a result change gears – from one where exploration, debate and pulling things apart and reassembling them are the main theme to one where synthesis, pulling things together and honing them into actions to be taken assume centre stage.

Chess masters know their opponents, not only by name but also by how they play – what their strengths are, where they are weak, the opportunities they offer through their

Chart 39 ***The Conversation Model – SWOT***

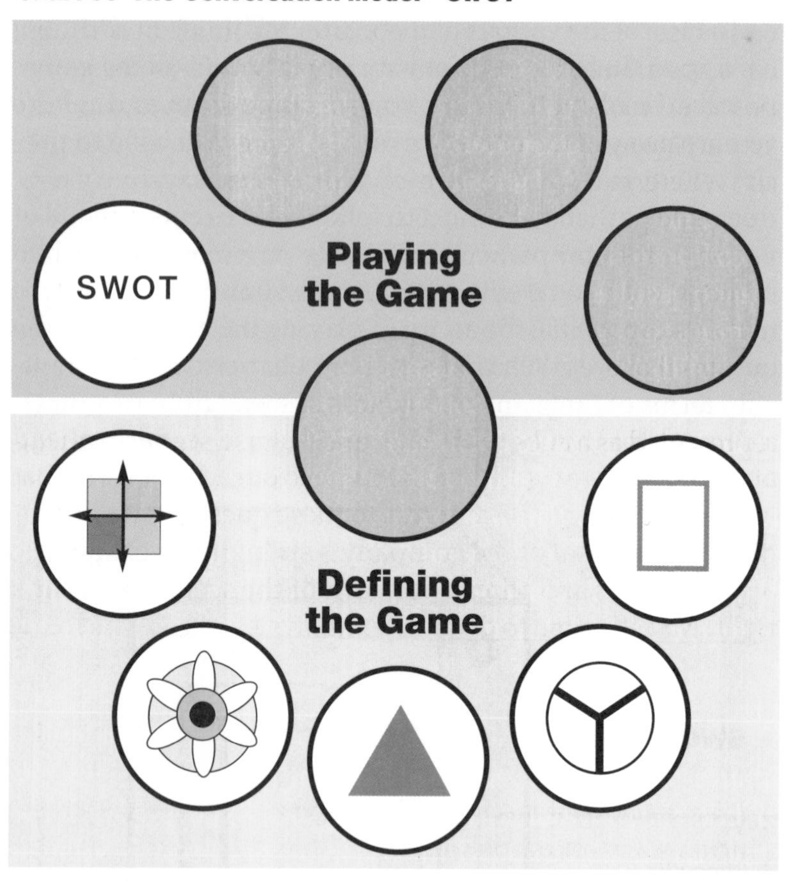

weaknesses and the threats they present because of their strengths. In essence, they do a SWOT analysis of themselves and their opponents before they play a game. In fact, this is a common part of the preparation programme in most sports at professional level and even at college and school.

SWOT is well understood in business, which is why it's a popular procedure for many companies. However, it is generally used in isolation as a strategic tool and is done by the company on itself. It therefore runs the risk of becoming yet another dot in space where its true value and potential can be lost. Used as part of the strategic conversation in the context of the game of business, a SWOT analysis becomes a powerful tool – it helps to bridge *defining* the game and the actual *playing* of the game. As such, it represents a shift in the conversation from elements outside of the company's control to things that the company *can* control. From this moment onwards the company begins to design its implementable strategy with SWOT crystallising a company's understanding of its capabilities. Thus, it prevents wasted time discussing options that are either undo-able or offer very little leverage.

In terms of the game of business, a SWOT analysis can be represented as a cube with inner and outer dimensions as follows:

Chart 40
The SWOT Cube

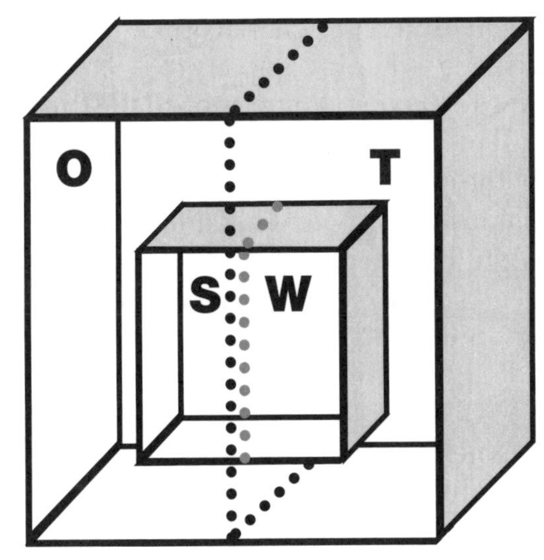

Key:

S Strengths
W Weaknesses
O Opportunities
T Threats

Strengths and weaknesses are inner dimensions because they are internal and relate to the core competencies of the company as well as to its culture, resources and even its business model and organisational structure. Opportunities and threats are external dimensions as they relate more to the key uncertainties within the business environment. Nevertheless, they should be more specific than the key uncertainties raised earlier in the conversation, since one is now interpreting the *consequences* of changes in the environment on the business in question.

Because of the external nature of opportunities and threats, most companies find them harder to identify in a standard SWOT analysis. They are further from home. However, once scenarios have been developed, the opportunities and threats become much clearer. Within the context of the game, opportunities may lead to a change in the scope of the game for a company, especially if they align with the company's core competencies. Or, vice versa, an expansion in product range or geographical scope may already have been discussed, in which case it represents an opportunity. Further on in the conversation, where a company can exploit an opportunity, it becomes an *option*. Equally, once the threats have been registered in terms of the game, it is easier for a company to identify the options needed to eliminate the threats or, at least, minimise their potential damage.

Astute readers will no doubt comment at this point: "But haven't we already visited our strengths, weaknesses, opportunities and threats?" Yes, when we examined the scope of the game, and especially when we looked at ourselves through the looking glass. Some elements of the SWOT analysis may have also been suggested earlier on in the process and recorded as IPAs – issues for potential action. By re-examining the insights gained during the earlier parts of the conversation, much of the SWOT analysis can be completed without difficulty. A bit of duplication doesn't do any harm. However, what often happens is that, when the company is brutally candid in its SWOT, it will sometimes identify discrepancies between how it initially perceived itself as a player in the game and the reality of its position given the range of scenarios. This means that a SWOT analysis should be conducted with a fresh mind (preferably after the tea interval).

Moreover, to be thorough, it should be conducted for each scenario on the gameboard, because a strength in one scenario can prove to be a fatal weakness in another. For example, a company which is the largest global producer of a particular commodity may benefit most in a strong market scenario: but that same company could be crippled in a weak market scenario if a large element of its production is coming from marginal ore bodies. Alternatively, in a very positive scenario for a country's economy, importers gain and exporters lose as a result of the appreciation of the local currency in international markets. Conversely, in a scenario where prospects are weak, exporters gain and importers lose as a result of the depreciation of the currency. In other words, one man's meat is another man's poison. A gameboard SWOT analysis can be tabulated as follows:

Chart 41 *The SWOT List*

Scenario	Strengths	Weaknesses	Opportunities	Threats
1				
2				
3				
4				

The usefulness of such a table is that, at a glance, it is possible to see in which scenario a company is best placed to operate. It also provides a comparative indication, based on a company's desired scenario as well as the scenario it feels will play out, of what kind of options are out there to remove threats and to capitalise on opportunities.

There are two ways in which you can take the SWOT process

a step further to achieve a better understanding of the risks in the game (and maybe secure a more influential position in playing it). Firstly, you can conduct a SWOT analysis on your main competitors; and, secondly, you can undertake a SWOT analysis on the principal players in your supply chain, both upstream and downstream. The first exercise emulates the chess master who studies his opponent, as we described at the beginning of this section. A SWOT analysis of your main competitors can prove invaluable in that it may give you a feel for how they would react to a change in scenarios and how you might outplay them in the changed game.

The second exercise reveals possible weak links in your chain. Often a switch in scenarios may be accompanied by changes in the rules of the game. Any player who does not or cannot adjust to the new rules (or the new scenarios) can disrupt the entire chain of supply. For instance, upstream you have to study the countries your suppliers are located in, on the grounds that should conditions turn ugly in any of those countries, there is precious little your supplier can do about it. Hence, an inherited weakness of your business is too much reliance on a supplier based in an unstable country or region. The same can apply to customers downstream. If you are dependent on a market that can disappear overnight for political or economic reasons, watch out.

It must be remembered that a SWOT analysis should never be a one-off, annual affair. Like a game of basketball or football, it should be done after every match (where in business a match is probably the quarterly results). The game of business requires regular conversation around a team's ongoing strengths, weaknesses, opportunities and threats as the season unfolds. That way the team is always re-examining and analysing its most effective options, which might just end up being the difference between winning and being runner-up in the league.

Options

There are moments in life
when the only possible option is to lose control.
PAULO COELHO

As players in any game we each play the game differently from each other. How we play the game is determined by our make-up. This means that consistency of play is a trademark

Chart 42 ***The Conversation Model – Options***

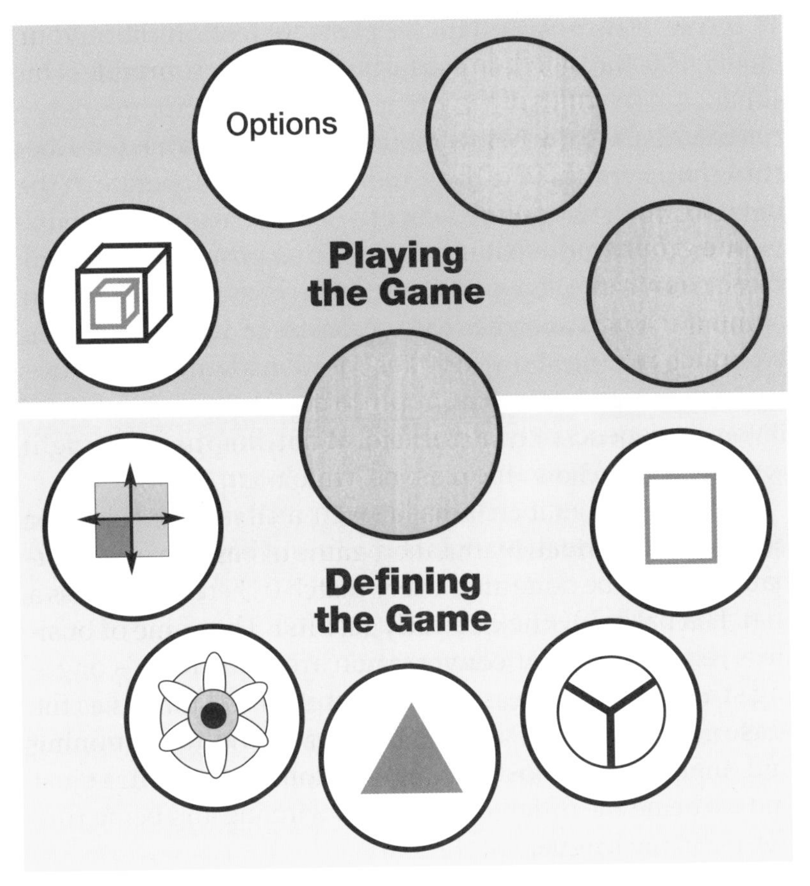

of most players and runs through the options they will choose. However, when the consistency of play becomes predictable, there is a risk that our competitors will anticipate our play, with the result that they gain competitive advantage.

Sometimes there is a need for players to change or adapt their game plan. In business, this means their business model. At this point of our process – after studying the scope of the game, the players, the rules of the game, the key uncertainties, the scenarios facing a company and its current strengths, weaknesses, opportunities and threats – a company is well qualified to examine carefully its business model in terms of its position in the game. Questions should be asked: Has the business model become too predictable? Has it become so set that it is difficult for the company to manoeuvre in the game? How robust is the business model? Does the company meet the basic requirements to operate in the game? Can the company look at options to enhance its business model? And what if the game changes, i.e. what if different scenarios play out? Does the business model give the company an advantage in each scenario, or does it need some tweaking or radical surgery? Decisions made around options will either support the status quo, or lead to the business model being adapted or transformed. Whatever the outcome, it will determine how the game is eventually played.

It is essential that option generation should be open and creative, and driven by three broad concerns:

1. Have the rules of the game, particularly the ones that are new, been taken into account?
2. Can the challenges faced by the key uncertainties be met?
3. Can the worst-case scenario be taken out of play and is it possible to move towards the best-case scenario?

With a clearer picture of the status of a company within the game and the influence of that company's business model (game plan) on the game, the company is now able to assess its most relevant overall strategy (i.e. the relevant strategic options) as follows:

1. If it is a strong player it should embark on a *growth strategy*, either through organic growth using options that tap into its core competencies; or through a stepping-out strategy that will take the company in a new direction; or,
2. If it is a competent player with a questionable future in the game because of its size or for other reasons, it should examine a *survival strategy*; or,
3. If its weaknesses and threats are overwhelming and it clearly has no future in the game, it should design the most economical *exit strategy*.

Remember those IPAs – the issues for potential action – that were generated throughout the process and 'banked' for further consideration? This is the stage of the process when they are generally discussed. In particular, possible new directions which may have emerged in the earlier debate on the scope of the game are 'stripped down' to a set of more realistic options. It may become clear, for example, that a previously suggested direction is not sensible in light of an uncertainty or scenario. Remember how you used to put together a jigsaw puzzle containing 500 pieces of an English countryside. You would start by removing all of the blue pieces to work on the sky first. In a similar way, the 'stripping down' process accelerates the building-up of a coherent picture of the options you really have available. This makes option generation easier and gives you a 'feel' for the possible outcomes of options before making any decisions. Obviously, as the construction of the puzzle proceeds, the interaction between the different elements of the overall scene begin to emerge, and will influence how the options are knitted together and prioritised.

With the 'puzzle' approach in mind, options can be considered from four different perspectives:

1. *Organic options*, where a company's core competencies are already strong and could therefore be used as a foundation for organic growth.
2. *Stepping-out options*, which may arise from the conversation around key uncertainties, with the resultant PI Chart showing that the company is more dependent on a particular product or market than it should be. It may involve a completely new direction for the business, or at least the exploration thereof. Caution should be exercised if this form of strategy is considered, as it possibly requires not only the development of new core competencies, but also a cultural shift within the company. Resource sufficiency and allocation would also need careful scrutiny.
3. *Generic options* are those that have to be pursued for all futures as a result of issues raised with regard to scope, players and changes in the rules of the game. If the company is not adhering to the descriptive and normative rules of the game, the generic options are quite clear: either obey the rules or get out of the game. Furthermore, the aspirational rules of the game (the rules to win) are the value drivers of the organisation. Specific focus should therefore be placed on options around these rules, as they form the basis of future growth strategies.
4. *Scenario-specific options* depend on which scenario is in play, e.g. options for survival in bad times like where to cut costs or close plants as against options in good times to expand the business, pay extra dividends to the

shareholders or both. Options arise out of events beyond our control and, as those events change, so do the options. Option generation that is specific to a particular scenario will equip a company with the necessary strategic and tactical 'fine-tuning' if and when that scenario unfolds. In each case, not only should the challenges posed by some of the key uncertainties with high impact potential be addressed; but the consequences of each option, especially in terms of the responses of other players in the game, also bear examination. If this is not done before any move is made, the end game may produce a result that is the exact opposite of what was desired. The company may then stumble over the unintended outcome and spend a great deal of its financial and human resources putting out the fire. Considering options for each scenario also gives the company a better 'feel' for which scenario it really would like to move towards in terms of its strategy, culture and purpose.

Let's move on to the subject of narrowing the options. Sometimes options sound great in conversation and, on the surface, seem like good choices; but on further analysis, they might not be the smartest choice. So how do we improve our understanding of the options so that we *can* make the smartest choice? Given that the descriptive rules of a game are the basic licence to operate, and the normative rules of the game are the moral rules of the game to which any world-class company must adhere; it makes sense that for any option to be effective it must not fall foul of either type of rule. We have therefore developed an Ethical Compass to be your guide (*Chart 43* overleaf).

An option that is between NW and NE on the Ethical Compass is both legal and moral and therefore safe to use. An option that hovers somewhere between NW and SW may be

Chart 43
The Ethical Compass

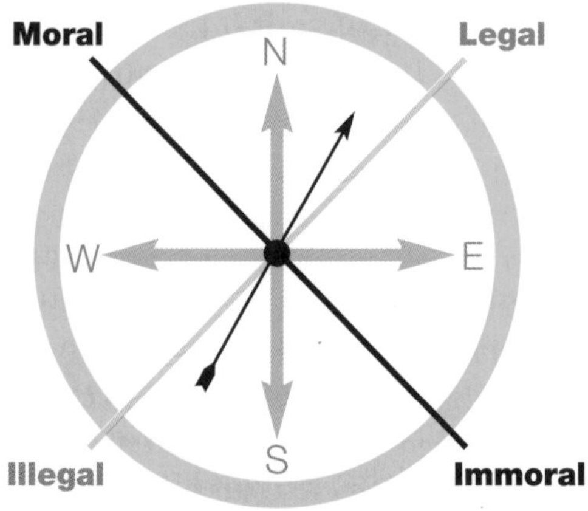

Moral
Legal
N
W
E
S
Illegal
Immoral

morally defensible, but it is illegal and therefore should only be taken if a crack legal team is on standby. This is often the game in dictatorship states with a poor record of human rights. It is clearly not a safe option, but one that may have to be taken in order to save one's corporate reputation. An option that is between NE and SE on the ethical compass will quite possibly raise the ire of other players, including consumer associations and other activist groups within the community, but will be easily defendable in court. An example of this is the option of outsourcing the manufacturing of designer label clothing to countries that allow family networks which may include child labour to do it. It may be legal in that country, but is it moral? Options of this nature may yield short-term gains but may prove unsustainable as part of a company's long-term strategy to be seen as a decent employer. Lastly, any option between SW and SE is both immoral and illegal. Any company implementing such an option will sooner or later go south. Do you recall Enron? How options are selected through the Ethical Compass will give you a good indication of what your meaning of 'winning' the game really is.

At this stage, we must raise the 'theory of tragic choices'. It states that not all choices in life are between good and evil; some are between good and lesser good (no problem for anyone) but some are between evil and greater evil. It is this last category that is the really tricky one. Nobody moral wants to do anything evil, but sometimes tragic consequences cannot be avoided. The US and Britain would argue that collateral damage in Iraq, which includes the loss of innocent civilian lives, should not deter the use of force to impose the greater good of freedom and democracy. We're in dangerous territory, because at what point does the level of inevitable (but unintended) evil more than offset the goal of greater good? When does the end no longer justify the means? The theory of tragic choices offers no precise answers, because there are none. But that statement in itself is crucial in differentiating hedgehogs from foxes. A hedgehog will follow his definition of good no matter what. Foxes will consider the consequences and maybe change their minds and follow a middle path. Hedgehogs will argue that this is not principled leadership. Foxes will respond that they believe in principles just as strongly as hedgehogs but *situational* leadership is better, i.e. the situation forms part of the decision. Fox-hunting has been finally banned in England and Wales after more than 300 years of the practice. The question is whether the adverse impact on rural communities will outweigh the obvious relief of foxes. Who's right? Who's wrong? As always, it depends on the situation and only time will tell.

Returning to the money side of the business, options can be subjected to further scrutiny by utilising what we call our Option Dartboard. No, it does not hang on the wall and it hasn't got a bull's-eye. But just as you throw a dart at a dartboard and receive a high or low score depending on where you land, so options can be graded too. The grading system revolves around the amount of resource input the option would demand in terms of money, people, time and the resultant level of output it may produce. The highest grade option would be one that requires little input but would, if successful, deliver an eminently high level of output. Pet names for this option include 'a quick win' and 'low-hanging fruit'. In contrast, any option that demands a high resource input but has little prospect of any significant output receives a low score (if it's not off the dartboard altogether). Most options fall somewhere between these two parameters and therefore can be pinned on the dartboard as indicated in *Chart 44*.

Safely assuming that most companies don't have an unlimited budget for the application of their strategy, any option that demands a high level of resource input is *exclusive* in that, by choosing it, the company has to refuse others. In other words, the company would be playing an 'either/or' game and there would be an opportunity cost involved. On the other hand, any option that requires low resource input needn't necessarily foreclose other options. It can therefore be considered *inclusive*, and the company would be in a position to play the 'and' game, i.e. it can pursue this and other options at the same time.

As a means of explanation we have plotted four options. Options 1 and 2 would each demand a high level of resource input to the extent that other options are excluded, with Option 1 offering the least output. Clearly not an attractive option. Options 3 and 4 on the other hand require less resource input each and permit you to do other things as well. Although Option 4 would require more input than Option 3, it does have the potential to generate a higher output. This would possibly make it a better option. The statement that strategy is as much about what you should *not* do as what you should do is only half true. It applies to exclusive, not inclusive options. Life is full of trade-offs, but sometimes it isn't: you can have it all.

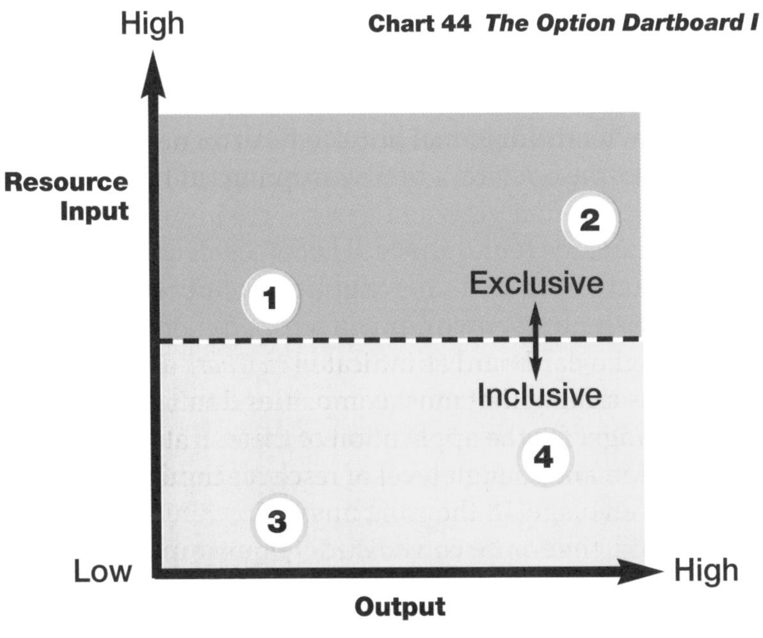
High
Chart 44 The Option Dartboard I
Resource Input
2
Exclusive
1
Inclusive
4
3
Low
High
Output

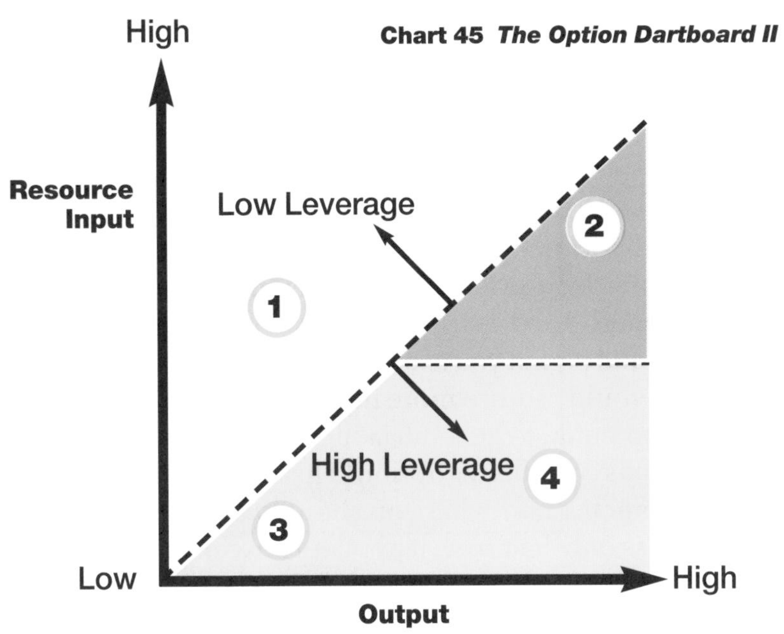
High
Chart 45 The Option Dartboard II
Resource Input
Low Leverage
2
1
High Leverage
4
3
Low
High
Output

The dartboard can be dissected in another way (as represented in *Chart 45* on the previous page). Based on resource input and output, some options have a higher degree of leverage than others. A diagonal line can be drawn on the board to represent the boundary between options of high and low leverage.

Using the same four options, it becomes clear that Option 1 is definitely not a first-choice option for any company, as it requires a high resource input in return for very low leverage in the game. The only time this option should be chosen is when the rules of the game require it, and the company has *no other option* if it wants to stay in the game. The area of safety is a case in point. Option 2 is an exclusive option but does have high leverage. In choosing this option, the opportunity costs would have to be considered. For example, choosing options 3 and 4 combined might be a better bet because they both possess high leverage as well.

Chart 46 ***The SHE Curve***

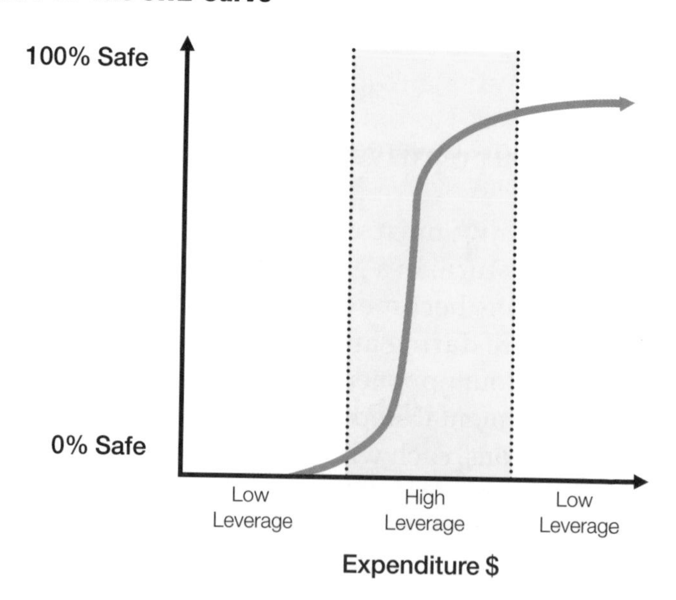

In companies where considerations of safety are paramount, a critical way to analyse options is in terms of the expenditure required to achieve an acceptable level of safety in the working environment. This relationship can be expressed as the SHE (safety, health, environment) curve in *Chart 46.*

In terms of the SHE curve, a minimum amount of expenditure is required to achieve any results at all. Below this amount, leverage is low to nil. There follows a band of expenditure within which options can produce a significant improvement in safety, the health of employees and conditions of the environment – up to as much as 95 per cent of what is possible. This is an area of high leverage. Beyond this, the remaining 5 per cent requires a huge amount of expenditure, with ever decreasing leverage. However, this last 5 per cent may be vital to prevent an accident which, even though it is extremely unlikely to happen, could result in a large loss of life if it does. Hence, an option should sometimes be chosen for reasons other than leverage. It's very hard, though, to take risk totally out of play, because it's more difficult to justify expenditure to stop something happening than to make something happen. Governments have the same problem with preventing terrorist acts. How much money and how many civil liberties are you prepared to sacrifice to make a country safe?

The nal matter we must cover in the option section centres on risk and return. In a game of chess, as each move is made new options become apparent. Some are entirely safe, but some are daring and might meet with an unexpected move by your opponent. The same is true in business where each incremental step in the decision-making chain unveils new options, each with its own risk/return profile. In a way, it's like placing bets. Depending on the magnitude of the bet, there is a level of risk beyond which you normally wouldn't go unless the bet was small or you were a real gambler. Similarly, in business, when judging an option such as whether or not to go ahead with a new project, a key factor to weigh up is the magnitude of the bet the company would be taking (i.e. the percentage of the company's assets or market capitalisation it would be putting on the table) versus the chance of unintended failure. Prudence dictates that the greater the magnitude of the bet, the safer the option has to be in order for it to be exercised. This principle, however, is broken time and again in corporate bidding wars, where risk rises in direct proportion to increases in the amount bid. The price just goes on up. But then takeover battles are about power and pride, and pride invariably comes before the fall.

The relationship between risk and return is shown in the R & R Graph *(Chart 47)*:

Chart 47
The R&R Graph

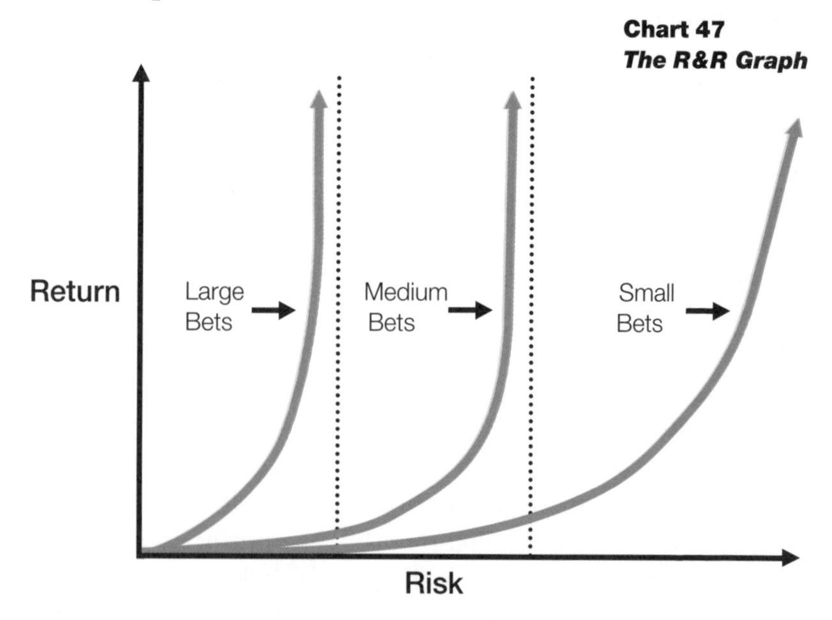

Applied within a business context, the terms used in this graph can be defined as follows:

1. The *magnitude of the bet* is the percentage of wealth you are willing to wager.
2. The *risk* is the chance of unintended failure due to market, cost, technical or political factors, or a combination thereof.
3. The *return* is the return on capital employed or the internal rate of return after discounting all future cash ows.

According to the R & R graph, there is a choke limit for options involving large and medium-sized bets (represented by the dotted line). No matter how high the anticipated return is, most companies will simply not go beyond a certain level of risk. For small bets, the risk is open-ended as long as the anticipated return rises in step with the risk. Obviously, choke limits vary from company to company, depending on how entrepreneurial the CEO and the board are. It is not unknown for a board to bet the entire company on a single project, but it's rare, and the company usually has to be in pretty desperate circumstances. In our conversations, we find the R & R chart is used sparingly, since the vast majority of options raised in a strategic conversation individually represent small percentages of a company's overall wealth. Nevertheless, the risk of an option has to be taken into account.

All companies have a limited amount of top management time and cannot waste it. Time is, after all, money. Generating options through strategic conversation provides informed choices and takes the guesswork out of strategy formulation. The best possible paths forward become clearer as the false leads are unveiled. We are not for one moment saying that an executive team should slog through every one of the charts we've inserted in this section. But the principles behind them should be kept in mind at all times. All that is required now is to make strategic decisions to take the company on the path with the greatest chance of winning the game.

Decisions

No sensible decision can be made any longer
without taking into account not only the world as it is,
but the world as it will be.

ISAAC ASIMOV

Decisions! Decisions! We only say that when we are caught between equally attractive options like which chocolate to

Chart 48 ***The Conversation Model – Decisions***

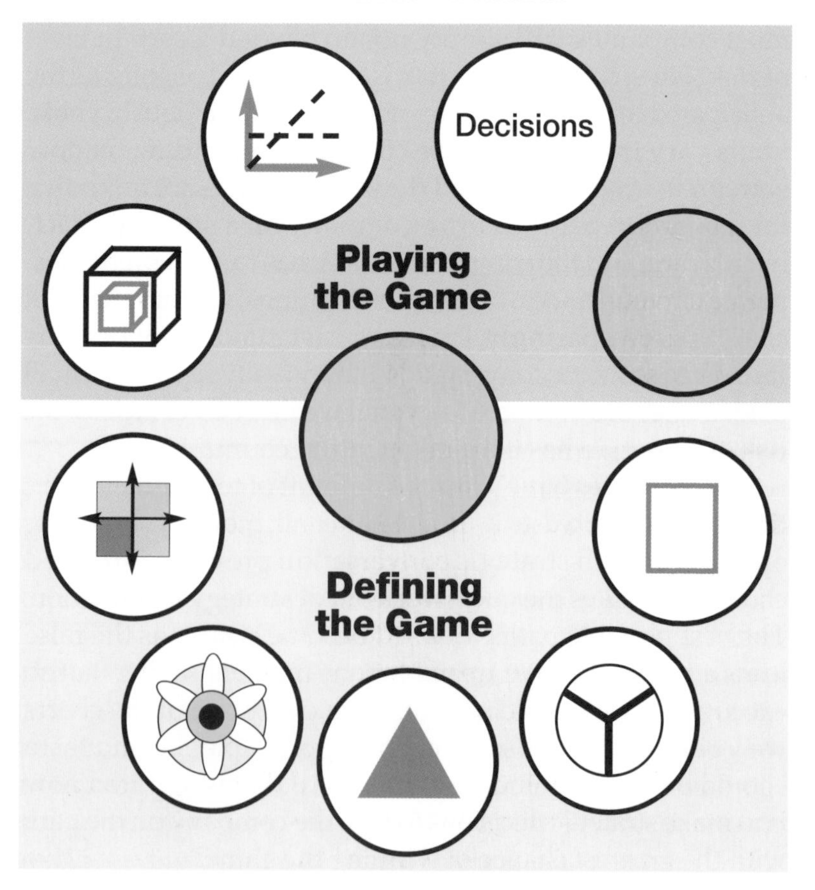

have in the box. Think about how many decisions we make in a day from the moment we open our eyes to when we close them. Life (when you're awake) is a continuous decision stream. And the difference between options and decisions is very simple. With options you can be as wild as you like because you are not making a commitment. With decisions you are committing yourself.

Nevertheless, the interesting thing is that you *only* have to make decisions when you *have* options. In prison, for example, you make very few decisions in a day, because you have very few options – dress, food and recreation periods are pretty much laid down. In the outside world, a routine job can mean you have very few options while you are doing it. You almost go into a decision-less mode, performing the routines like an unthinking robot. Sadly, the poorer you are, the fewer options you have. If you have one skirt or one pair of trousers, you don't have to make decisions when you dress. At the other end of the scale, if you're very, very rich, your options become endless. Want a candle-lit dinner in New York when you're shopping in Paris in the morning? Just ring up the pilots of your private jet and ask them to fire the engines up because you'll be at the airport in the next hour. This all boils down to one inescapable fact: you should really only entertain options that you have the capability of turning into action. Otherwise, it's daydreaming. So check your span of control before making any decision.

In the context of this phase of the strategic conversation, we must return to another distinction we made at the beginning of the book – the difference between strategic and tactical decisions. Strategic decisions are ones which change the direction of your life; tactical decisions are the ones you make every day to stay alive. Your parents make some strategic decisions on your behalf – like having you in the first place! Seriously though, they decide on the neighbourhood where you're brought up, the school in which you are enrolled and to some extent the value system you take through life. Then you take over and start making strategic decisions on whether or not to attend university, which career to choose, where you are going to live and with whom you are going to hitch a ride in the longer run (the other option: staying single). The important thing to realise is that if you accept this definition of 'strategic', you don't often make strategic decisions – maybe fewer than a hundred in your life. Some people will argue that this is too narrow a definition. But we're into semantics. Sure, you may want to cast a wider net for classifying decisions as strategic, but the main point still stands: strategy is about direction, tactics is about how to get there.

So how do we transfer all the thoughts we've expressed about making decisions in our personal lives to the world of business? According to the definition we've accorded to the term 'strategic', the only part of the conversation model around which decisions can be called truly strategic is the scope of the game. If your business significantly expands its product range or replaces existing products with new and different ones, that can be considered a change of direction and is often referred to as 'strategic repositioning'. If you take over another company (or start a business from scratch) in an entirely new field, that is likewise a strategic decision. Moving into a new country in a major way, same deal. By contrast, gradual organic growth of a business where internal research and development leads to a steady stream of new and upgraded versions of your existing product range would fall into the 'tactical' classification – innovation to keep yourself alive. Major decisions about organisational structure, human resource policies, nancial/IT systems and capital structure would also be tactical. Decisions about the business model can go either way depending on the magnitude of the decision.

Does this mean that strategic conversations should not embrace all these issues? Absolutely not. As we said at the outset, our conversation model should be seen as a prelude to the normal planning cycle. Thus, it must include both strategic and tactical decisions so that one segues in a logical fashion from the big picture of strategy to the more detailed arena of tactics. Moreover, the whole purpose of introducing key uncertainties and the scenario gameboard into the conversation is to explore how tactics need to be adapted in order to cope with possible changes in the environment. Added to which, radical external shifts may demand a revamp of strategy like redirecting your game, exiting part of it or closing up shop altogether.

Ultimately, the quality of strategic conversation is defined by the calibre of decisions that are made as a result of it. But this is not the end of it. Some of these decisions then have to be converted immediately and some stockpiled in case there are changes in the environment. As in any game, players in business work strategically to create opportunities and to counter threats. Often though, there's no implementation of the decisions, i.e. no action, and then the opportunity is lost or the threat grows. It is therefore a vital step in our model that decisions from the range of options are banked for action today or possible action tomorrow. But which option is the right one to select? The secret here is to identify which of the scenarios is most likely to play out. This decision alone will form the basis of the company's five-year plan and accompanying budget. Obviously, if the future changes within the realm of the scenario gameboard, the strategy will be revisited and adjusted accordingly. If, however, the future changes dramatically in a direction totally unexpected, the scenario gameboard, options and decisions will have to be re-examined in a new round of strategic conversations.

In today's business world where global connectivity punishes you very quickly for procrastination, there is an emphasis on policy execution. We are, in fact, entering an 'era of policy execution'. A company's success or failure in the global market can sometimes be measured within days of the execution of its strategy. If it wants to remain a player in the game, more than ever before a company has to update its understanding continually of the subtle shifts taking place on the field. A foxy company adapts its execution of strategy in light of its opponents' tactics and other twists in the plot beyond its control.

In the fantasy world of action movies, the hero always ends up in a situation where he has to make one of two decisions: save the girl or save the world. And somewhere nearby there will always be a large bomb with a clearly visible digital timer ticking away. Whichever choice he makes he risks a negative outcome. It's obvious that, given the choice, the hero would clearly prefer not to be in the situation, and the suggestion is that the decision he has to make is forced onto him by factors outside of his control. Of course, we momentarily forget that our hero has superpowers and will therefore easily manage to save the girl (and everyone else), defuse the bomb and beat up the baddy, all without disturbing the parting in his hair.

In the real world, decision-making is a fundamental life skill and not simply an act of choosing the most appealing option; and unfortunately not enough emphasis is placed on this skill within the whole strategic process. Often a decision is made at the end of a strategic process that is out of the context with the whole game. It is frequently based on an arbitrary response to a situation, or is blurred by emotion and, especially in business, by power plays and personal attachments. Although these factors cannot be ignored, because they are, whether we like it or not, elements in any decision-making process; they can destroy value in the chain when they become too dominant. The effect is to steer the company in the wrong direction or in no direction at all. Jamaicans have a typically vivid expression for this predicament: "sitting on the one-one cocoa" – a wooden raft that cannot be steered but instead see-saws with the waves, moving backwards and forwards and not really going anywhere. How many company chairmen sit on their one-one chairs performing the same aimless role?

As we know, a philosophy of doubt and indecision doesn't work in business. Decisions need to be made, deadlines have to be met. Straddling the fence can lead to very painful results. Because effective decision-making relies on both intuitive and analytical thought, it is an art as well as a science. It is not simply about making a choice. It's about *creating* choice within your span of control and then deciding from that choice. And obviously with a little help from your friends, you can widen your span of control. Alliances and partnerships are formed on that basis. Whereas some decisions are no-brainers and therefore require very little exercising of any decision-making skills, most of the important decisions we make are complex. They will have outcomes, both expected and unexpected. In the game of business, strategic decisions made by any player in the game will have an impact on the game. Other players will react and the game will change.

Because companies are people organisations, decisions will also affect people within the company; and because people are sensitive and emotional they will react, sometimes illogically. No matter how much a company develops a team-playing ethos, every player within the team will eventually do whatever is necessary to protect his or her own interest. So, the bigger the company, the more complex the decisions and outcomes, and the more necessary it is to have the kind of strategic conversation we have outlined. It allows a company to look through the lens of complexity, understand the game better and make the most effective incremental decisions in a process that has a built-in mechanism for adaptation. By making decisions around scenarios, you can adjust gradually to a changing environment rather than having to make dramatic switches. Implementing our conversation model gives people the ability to learn how to make better decisions by interaction with their colleagues. The more the model is used and the more iterative it is, the greater the degree of mutual learning and frequency of breakthroughs.

By the time the application of the model has got to the decision phase, the correct problems have been identified and clearer objectives have emerged. Clarity on key uncertainties and alternative futures through scenario construction has instilled more flexibility in the nature of decision-making. It has also developed the mindset that mistakes are part of the learning process and that better decisions are made when creative thought to overcome a weakness is harnessed. Furthermore, the model discloses a company's appetite for risk. It compels consideration of where decisions might lead in the future and therefore provides a deeper understanding of any difficult choices and trade-offs down the line. Above all, the model encourages an examination of the potential outcomes of any decision.

Decision-making can lead to three types of outcomes:

- an intended outcome (IO);
- an unintended outcome (UO);
- a zero outcome (OO).

This is represented in *Chart 49*.

Even though a company's strategy is to get from A to B, the tactical decisions needed to steer it there will need to be broken down into do-able chunks, first to establish momentum and then to build upon that momentum. Each tactical decision is based on the outcome of the previous decision, which is either intended or unintended.

Should a decision have an intended outcome, the next decision made will simply be in line with the original, or planned, overall decision. It could be slightly different from the first decision, depending on the circumstances and the response to the first decision (hence the adjacent circles), but it will still be in line with the overall strategy.

Chart 49
The Decision Tree

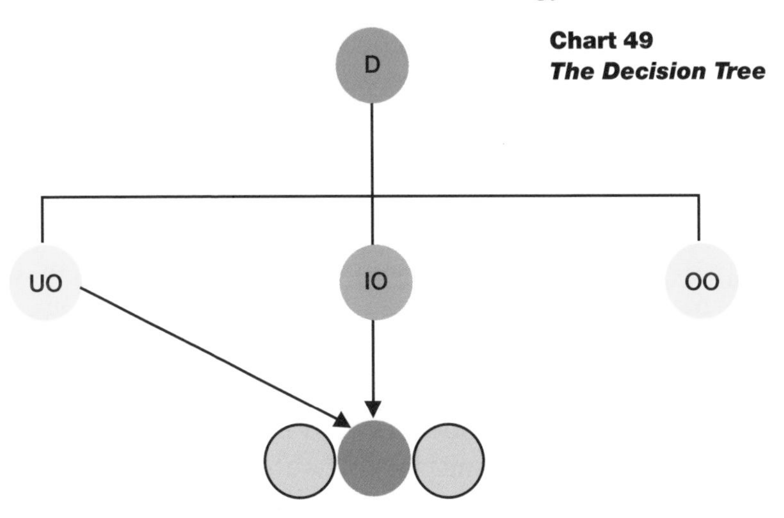

If, however, a decision produces an unintended outcome, it is crucial to examine *why* there was an unintended outcome if any degree of learning is to take place. Anyone who has hit their thumb with a hammer instead of hitting a nail will agree that it was an unintended outcome and that unless they examine a possible reason for this happening, it could very easily happen again. In another context, an iron shot that completely misses the green can be viewed as an unintended outcome in a game of golf. It could be the result of incorrect implementation – something within the player's control to rectify like an incorrect grip, stance or swing. If, on the other hand, a gust of wind deflected the ball in flight from its intended direction, it might be the fault of the player because he should have checked the wind; or it might not be his fault because the gust happened out of the blue. Either way, his next shot is like the diagonal arrow in our diagram, a do-able thing to get back on track.

In business, the sign of a successful strategic conversation is one where an unintended outcome has already been worked through and the tactics are adjusted accordingly. Catch-up is easy. A zero outcome is the result of finger problems or lack of follow-through (as opposed to a decision to do nothing).

Unlike a game of chess where decisions can be turned into action very quickly by the player simply moving a piece on the board, the implementation of a decision in business requires a whole set of actions to be taken by management and staff working in concert. Because people tend to make more effort in getting things done if they know their results are going to be measured, a zero outcome is less likely in a situation where outcomes are being measured. Hence, the second last step in our conversation model is to establish measurable outcomes. Indeed, a measurable outcome of the decision phase of the conversation should be a ranking of decisions in terms of importance and urgency, as well as a list of options rejected or held over for later consideration.

Incidentally, a little known fact about the spectacular turnaround in the crime rate in New York is that it wasn't just due to the 'broken window' strategy of following up on the most trivial of crimes. It was also attributable to CompStat – a computer system which tracked all categories of crime on a weekly basis in each precinct. Where there was an increase in a particular category, in a particular precinct, the police chief was called to account. If he complained about lack of resources, he was given extra ones. If at subsequent meetings the statistic was still heading in the wrong direction, he was replaced. Simple, no nonsense stuff. It should be used in every city with a crime problem.

Measurable Outcomes

There are two possible outcomes:
if the result confirms the hypothesis,
then you've made a discovery.
If the result is contrary to the hypothesis,
then you've made a discovery.

ENRICO FERMI
Nobel prize-winning physicist

As we were at pains to point out earlier on, without measurable outcomes, conversations are social, not strategic. Asking attractive strangers at a function how they are is polite and sociable. Asking those same persons for their telephone number is strategic. It has a measurable outcome: they either give it or they don't. If the response is affirmative, it implies permission to make further contact with the promise of maybe a series of increasingly elevated measurable outcomes. We will introduce you to our incremental staircase in a minute.

Because of the interactive nature of the business game, the larger its scope and the longer its duration the less control a player can have over its outcome. For this reason, short-term strategy – which in our nomenclature may be more accurately described as tactics – can have clear measurable outcomes. It is easier to budget for, and easier to monitor. Suppose, therefore, you have chosen a strategic option. To get the show on the road, you need to identify a nice, easy, initial task and ask yourself: who is going to do what, by when, and how much is it going to cost? The answers to these questions can be inserted among the targets, milestones and key performance indicators normally included in the one-year operational plan against which progress is monitored on a monthly or quarterly basis. One of the commonest first steps we have come across in our experience of facilitation is merely to evaluate

Chart 50 ***The Conversation Model – Measurable Outcomes***

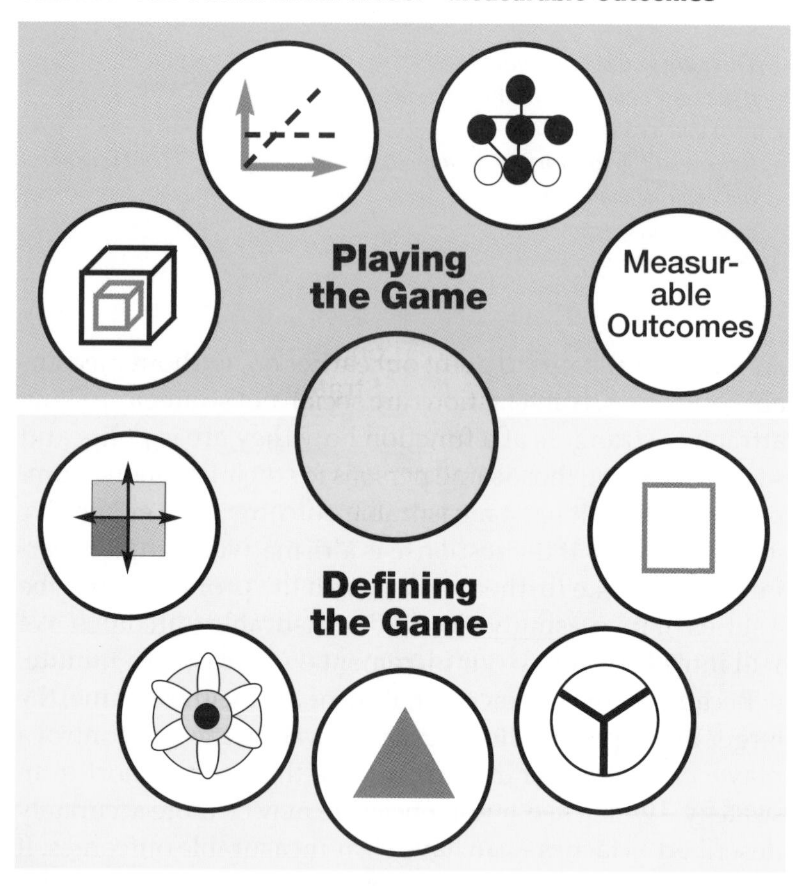

the option in more detail. That's fine. Reintroducing our cone of uncertainty, the conversation on short-term strategy falls on the left-hand side of the diagram *(Chart 51* opposite).

Over time, the cone of uncertainty widens as more and more factors beyond our control influence developments. More and more flags are needed to monitor developments and ensure some measure of control. Long-term strategy therefore is not as clear cut as short-term strategy. While there may be a grand, eventual outcome, getting there requires

Chart 51 ***The Cone of Uncertainty II***

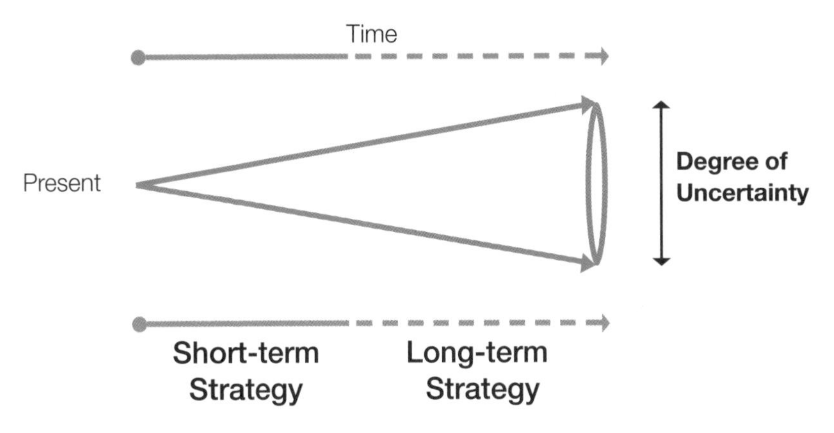

more flexibility. Therefore, true success can usually only come about by establishing a series of outcomes upon which the strategy is incrementally built. Detractors of incremental decision-making will argue that you can't cross a chasm with anything but a single jump. Our comment would be that if you are faced with a chasm, then you probably haven't strategised properly. Just once in a while, you have to take a mighty leap (preferably with a bungee cord attached).

Chart 52 ***The Incremental Staircase I***

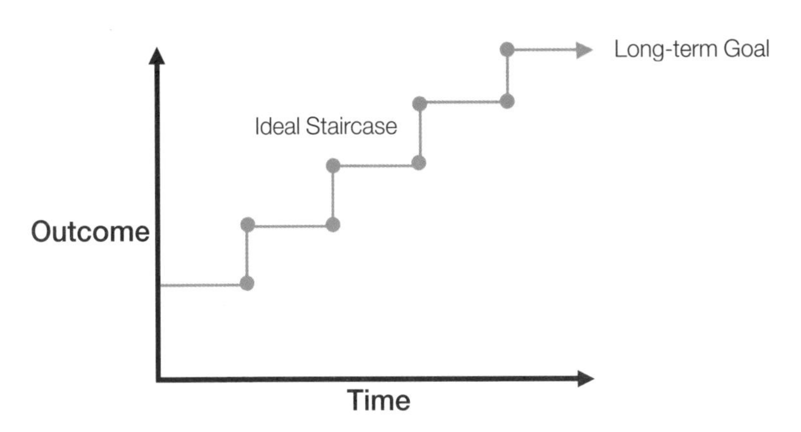

Thus, our recommended approach to long-term strategy is akin to climbing a staircase similar to the one in *Chart 52*.

However, this is an ideal staircase where each step propels you upward and is of the same height. In the real world, external events beyond the control of a company often change the shape and direction of the staircase. Victories and setbacks mean that it looks more like this:

Chart 53 ***The Incremental Staircase II***

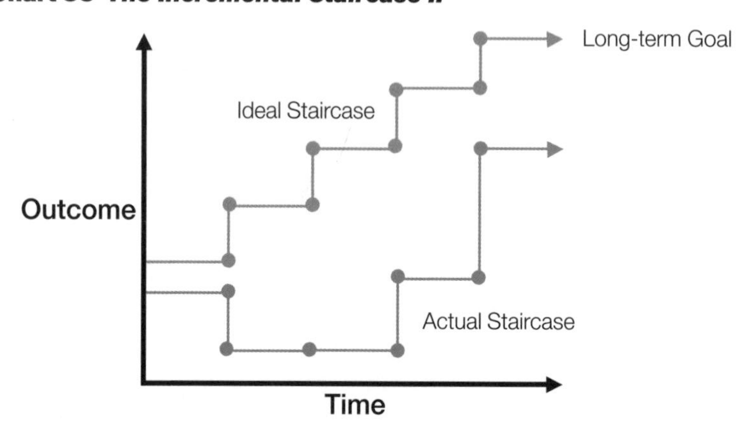

The objective is still to reach your goal. It just might take you a little longer to get there (although sometimes with the wind behind you, you arrive early). The best example we can quote you is the English Premier League for soccer. Unless you're Arsenal in the 2003/4 season, you're bound to lose the odd match (represented by a downward step). Draws move you sideways and wins take you up a notch. The real point is that it doesn't matter what the final shape of your ladder is, as long as it is higher than that of any other soccer team in the league. For that is what wins you the cup. In business, the same principle applies. It's not about perfection. It's about beating your competitors, which is an appropriate way of introducing the last step in our conversation model – the meaning of winning.

The Meaning of Winning

If the world be worth thy winning,
Think, oh think, it worth enjoying.
JOHN DRYDEN

The ultimate step in our conversation model is to make sense of what it means to win the game. If the meaning of winning for a company is purely about chasing targets, it has already

Chart 54 ***The Conversation Model – Meaning of Winning***

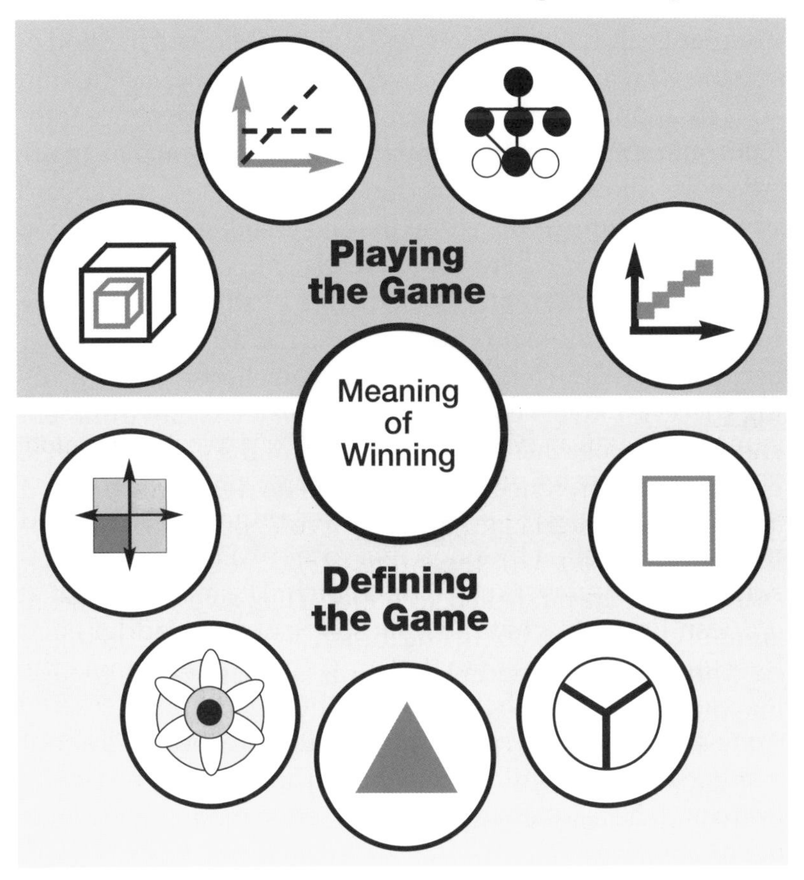

lost the game. Yes, measuring the performance of people against targets has its place (as we've already remarked), but dots don't mean anything if they're not put in context. Have you ever gone around the factory floor asking employees why the company exists and why they're doing what they're doing? You'd be surprised by the variety of answers, some of which would be revelations. People need a purpose, an end; and if you don't provide them with one, the vacuum will be completely taken up by their own purposes and ends.

A game of sport has a start and an end. It sometimes has a distinct time period (ninety minutes plus injury time for Premier League soccer matches) and sometimes a method of scoring which determines how long a match will last (tennis, squash, snooker, darts). Sometimes it's about distance (athletics) and sometimes the number of holes that you play (golf). All sports, though, share one thing in common – a scoreboard or scorecard which tells you at the end whether you won, you lost, you drew or where you were placed.

Business is different. A sustainable business has no time frame and therefore no end. Business has no overall winner because it all depends on the dates you choose for measuring success. Players come and go, the external environment shifts and sometimes even the nature of the game changes. But the real difference is that there is no definite scorecard and no exact criteria laid down in a rulebook for determining whether you won the game. "Oh," you might object, "what about the published accounts? They give you the score annually." They do, but in one dimension. "Well," you might continue, "the business of business is business. So the bottom line profit *is* the score."

Hmm, let's explore that philosophically.

If we wish to win in the game, we need to ask ourselves a very obvious, yet powerful, question: "What is *our* meaning of winning?" For example, is it to:

- be the employer of choice?
- be the supplier of choice?
- be the most admired company by the public/customers?
- win the 'green' award for triple bottom-line achievement?
- grow our earnings per share and share price ahead of our competitors?
- be the industry innovator?
- etc.

A hedgehog approach to the meaning of winning is equivalent to staring down a telescope – one lens offering one vision. Mine! So all we have to do is identify an optimal strategy in order to win the game according to *my* definition: Simple. You don't have to make any decisions in this regard because you have no option. There are plenty of CEOs turned astronomers out there who think this is the way to go.

Chart 55 ***The Kaleidoscope of Winning***

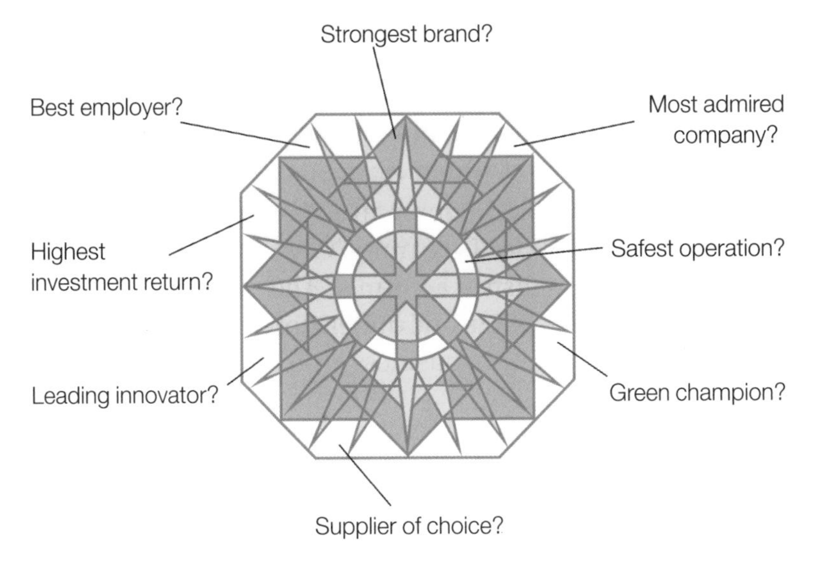

In counterpoint, the games that foxes play present a variety of ways to win. They look at the meaning of winning not through a telescope, but through a kaleidoscope *(Chart 55)*. The mirrors create different views of an ever-changing picture of the future. Because a company is a social organisation, the different people that make it up have different wishes, different opinions, different strengths and weaknesses. There is no single meaning of winning. A successful strategy is articulated through a balance of each person's meaning of winning. A sustainable business therefore emerges not from seeking alignment of everyone's meaning of winning, but a *balance* between their meanings, i.e. achieving a win over a variety of fronts instead of aiming for a single win.

How do we go about extracting these personal views of winning at the tail end of the strategic conversation? We literally go around the table individual by individual and ask them where they'd like to see the company in five years' time. What prize would they want the company to win? It's amazing how everyone's eyes light up as they articulate their desire for the company. And the soft factors to do with respect and decency feature more prominently than you might expect (our answer to the bottom-liners). We faithfully transcribe what they say onto a flip chart and carefully hand over the sheets to be framed and hung up in the corridors of power for all to see. In addition, we strongly advocate that they form the basis of the company's vision and mission statement – if the company desires to have one. It's better than the usual corporate homily of hollow-sounding platitudes. The objectives are real.

You may find this final step a little too disruptive for your liking. But what makes a winning organisation? Surely it's not perfect alignment. It's more a case of building a common purpose out of the diversity that exists around you. A diamond would not be a diamond if it had only one facet.

Full House

The sleeping fox catches no poultry.

BENJAMIN FRANKLIN

There you have it. We have laid down our cards (except for three still up our sleeve). It's a full house. The diagram looks a bit like an Egyptian hieroglyph but there is no other like it in the world. Indeed, our model completely upends many of

Chart 56 ***The Conversation Model – Full House***

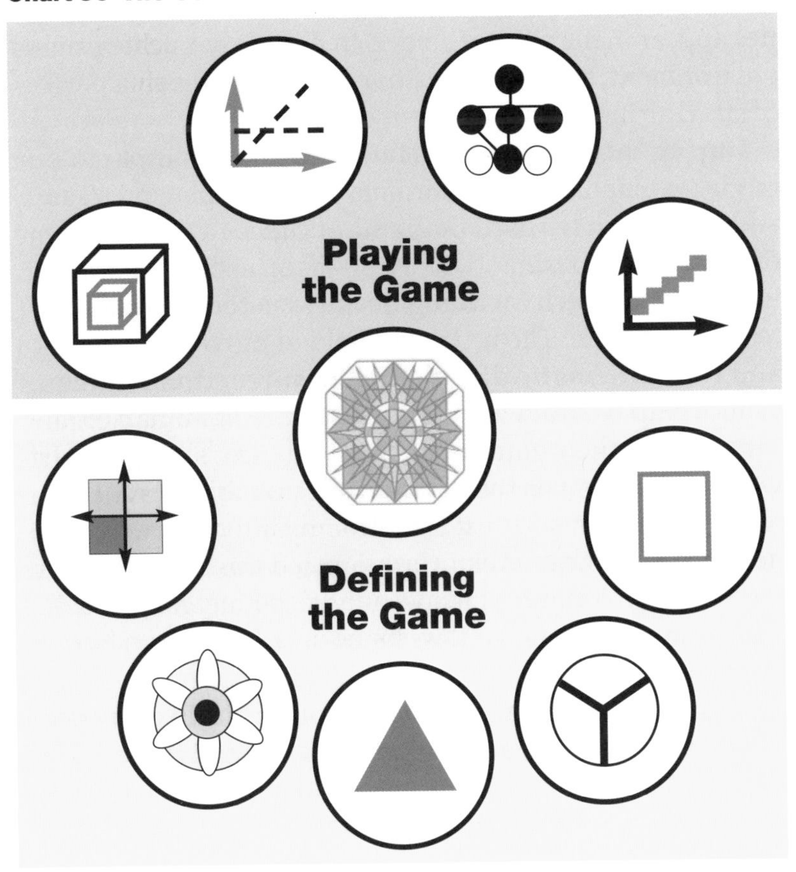

the models on display in academic circles. No doubt in the fullness of time, someone will come along with something smarter and take out our 'full house' with 'four of a kind'. Great – but we don't see our basic logic being disturbed. The transformation of global business is unfolding before our very eyes. Today's future is tomorrow's history. Over the past decade and a half, the explosion of the internet has added new impetus to globalisation and, paradoxically, the increasing connectivity has cast a growing shadow of uncertainty over the way we do business. Although increased access means that more is known now than ever before, uncertainties appear in the blink of an eye. In this hurly-burly business environment, many companies need a more flexible process of strategising simply to survive.

During the course of this book, we have compared our model of planning in extraordinary times to playing a game. Although we have used the game of chess – a popular game of strategy in Russia and the West – as an analogy at times, it is clearly no match for doing business in the uncertainty of today's markets. The restricted field of movement in chess and its mathematically based action-reaction strategies cannot help us deal with the complexities of human organisations and their emotional and sometimes illogical drivers. In reality, given the innumerable possible permutations of the game of business, it is more similar to the ancient Chinese board game of Weiqi (pronounced *wai-chi*), otherwise known as Go (from the Japanese character meaning *battle*). It is a game that predates chess by close on a thousand years. The concept of the game is relatively simple: two players each place stones (one player white, the other black) on various intersecting points of a 19 x 19 grid. The object is to surround and isolate connections between an opponent's adjacent stones and thereby limit any territorial growth and advantage. Because it is a large board and rules are somewhat limited, it allows great scope in strategy. What's more, decisions in one part of the board are influenced by situations that develop on other parts of the board, and moves made at the beginning of the game can have consequences hundreds of moves later on.

The scope of the game is too large to imagine. In fact, it's been calculated that, given the size of the board and the limited restrictions, there are approximately 2.1×10^{170} possible combinations of positions in a game of Weiqi as opposed to between 10^{43} and 10^{50} in the game of chess. To put things further into perspective, some physicists estimate that there are fewer than 10^{90} protons in the entire visible universe!

The emphasis in Weiqi is on the importance of balancing tensions at different levels within the game. To secure an area of the board requires moves that are close together; and yet to cover the largest territory possible a player needs to spread out. To ensure that you do not fall behind, you need to play aggressively; but playing too aggressively leaves weaknesses undefended that can be exploited. Playing too close to the edge secures insufficient territory and minimal growth; yet diversifying too far from the edge opens a player up to invasion. Does sound a bit like business, doesn't it? Western companies wishing to operate in China would do well to remember this. It's a whole new game that requires different strategic thinking and a different meaning of winning. Indeed, one of the differences between the concept of the future possessed by Chinese and Americans is that the Chinese think it will change whereas Americans think it will get better.

If we are to attempt to strategise in a game under such extraordinary conditions, the best we can do is acquire a detailed understanding of the game and its players, as well as to effect an honest self-appraisal; eliminate those elements which will have little or no impact on the future, and then prioritise what remains in the design of possible scenarios.

By doing so, it is possible to extrapolate a full range of options and then make decisions that can be constantly measured and assessed for their effectiveness.

Generally, executive teams spend too much time discussing tactics under the banner of strategy and not enough time on developing clear strategic direction for the company. The conversation model is an ideal methodology for allowing a high level of strategic conversation before moving into traditional strategic planning and tactical sessions. Furthermore, the process can take as little as five hours and at the most two days.

If a successful company is one that draws on the combined meanings of winning of all its significant internal players, it makes sense that its strategic direction should be formulated and driven by these same drivers. A strategic conversation should therefore be flexible enough to encourage the sharing of this diversity of insights and the nurturing thereof, and yet at the same time be sufficiently structured to facilitate its flow. We feel strongly that such a strategic conversation worked through the conversation model is an ideal tool for top and middle management to identify the direction in which the company and its workforce should travel if they wish to win the game.

Furthermore, the conversation, if cascaded down to the shop floor, provides a sense of purpose at every level. Because employees all take part in the process, it encourages buy-in. This in turn provides the necessary motivation to turn the plan into action. Out of the debate around the meaning of winning comes a feeling of common purpose. Anyone who has watched a children's swimming gala is well aware of the different ethos driving an individual and a house/team event. With the common purpose of the latter, there is a shared enthusiasm and energetic support from all involved, resulting in an increase in performance by individuals because they don't want to let the team down. Additionally, people who normally wouldn't shine on their own, and are aware of that, have an increased opportunity of experiencing the meaning of winning as part of the team.

Now for the three cards still up our sleeve. It would be remiss of us in our concluding remarks if we did not include three more examples of gameboards that we have found particularly popular over the past couple of years:

HIV/AIDS in South Africa

We have both had the benefit of giving presentations to very knowledgeable people in the field of HIV/AIDS who in turn have influenced the shape of our presentation.

We are in a war situation in South Africa where the HIV/AIDS virus is our very own micro weapon of mass destruction. To try to get people to understand the seriousness of this war and to show that there is a path to victory, we developed the following gameboard:

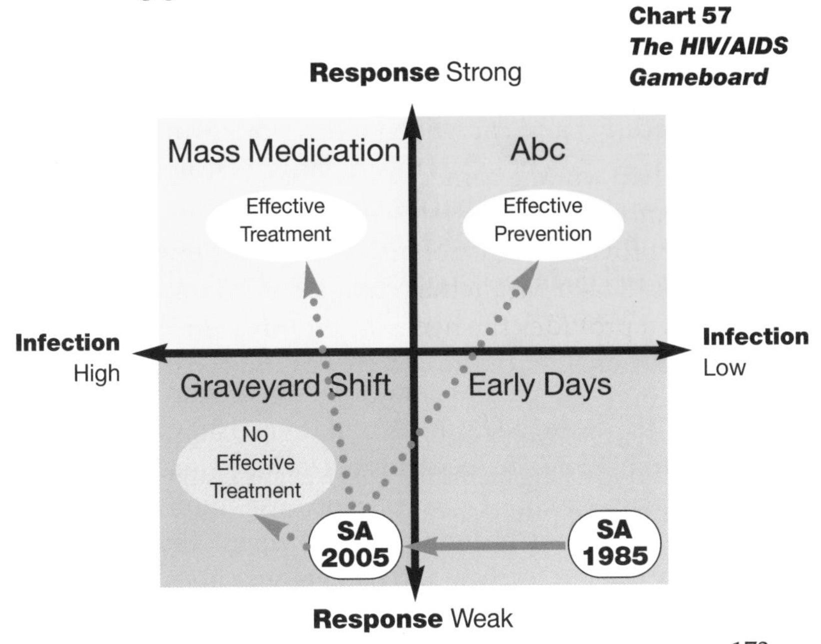

Chart 57
The HIV/AIDS Gameboard

In the *Early Days* scenario, the prevalence rate for HIV/AIDS is less than one per cent of the population. There are still isolated communities within South Africa that are in this scenario. But the bulk of the country moved out of this scenario by the mid-1990s.

Indeed, South Africa has just entered the *Graveyard Shift*, since the people infected in the mid-1990s are now dying of AIDS. The total number of registered deaths in the 30–34 age group is now higher than in any other age group for both males and females. This means that South Africa is losing its active working population as well as its parents, and leaving behind orphans and the elderly. If an effective treatment is not implemented, South Africa will sink deeper into the *Graveyard Shift*.

In the *Mass Medication* scenario, the government lives up to its promise of providing universal anti-retroviral treatment. An estimated five million people are eventually on medication, which makes it the largest programme of its kind in the world. Clinics are provided in every town and village to test for HIV and dispense the pills. The local doctors and nurses have access to HIV specialists for advice on each patient's treatment and care. Even if drug prices and medical overheads per patient fall as the initiative is scaled up, it is a very expensive scenario that also poses high risks. For if people don't comply fully with their treatment regimens, there is an increased chance of a resistant virus spreading, which will nullify the effectiveness of the whole programme. A vaccine remains a *wild card*.

The *Abc* scenario gets its name from the slogan: "Abstain; if you can't abstain, be faithful; and if you can't be faithful use a condom!" The *Abc* scenario is in fact the Ugandan model, which places greatest emphasis on abstention (hence the capital 'A' and small 'b' and 'c'). Government, the churches, community leaders, teachers and parents have urged teenagers to postpone their first sexual experience and then remain faithful to one partner. The programme, according to research conducted in Uganda, has achieved widespread behavioural change and lowered the teenage HIV prevalence rate.

The simple message of this gameboard for South Africa is that if it seriously enters the *Mass Medication* scenario (which we fully support), it must at the same time move into the *Abc* scenario. Otherwise, new infections could build the figure of five million to a much higher figure (assuming that anti-retrovirals slow down the AIDS death rate), which in turn will put even more strain on government financing of health care. However, for an *Abc* campaign to be effective, it will require a co-ordinated and passionate effort by all sectors of society, including the churches. Advertising agencies should be at the forefront of designing the campaign since it is their job to change people's behaviour.

The Ultimate Gameboard

It would be true to say that although HIV/AIDS dominates the scene in South Africa and many other developing countries, the developed world has other worries on its plate. Given the tempestuous nature of man, and his propensity for fighting, our world has been, and always will be, pockmarked with skirmishes, battles and wars that dictate the course of history. But there is one threat that is of global significance. It is well known that the current nuclear weapon stockpiles of the few nations who have them are enough to destroy all life on this planet many times over. The future of our existence hangs in the balance, because access to these weapons could dramatically increase over the next fifty years.

We have therefore constructed a gameboard which has peace and war as the horizontal axis and nukes and no nukes on the vertical axis.

This leads to four possible scenarios upon which we have

Chart 58 ***The Ultimate Gameboard***

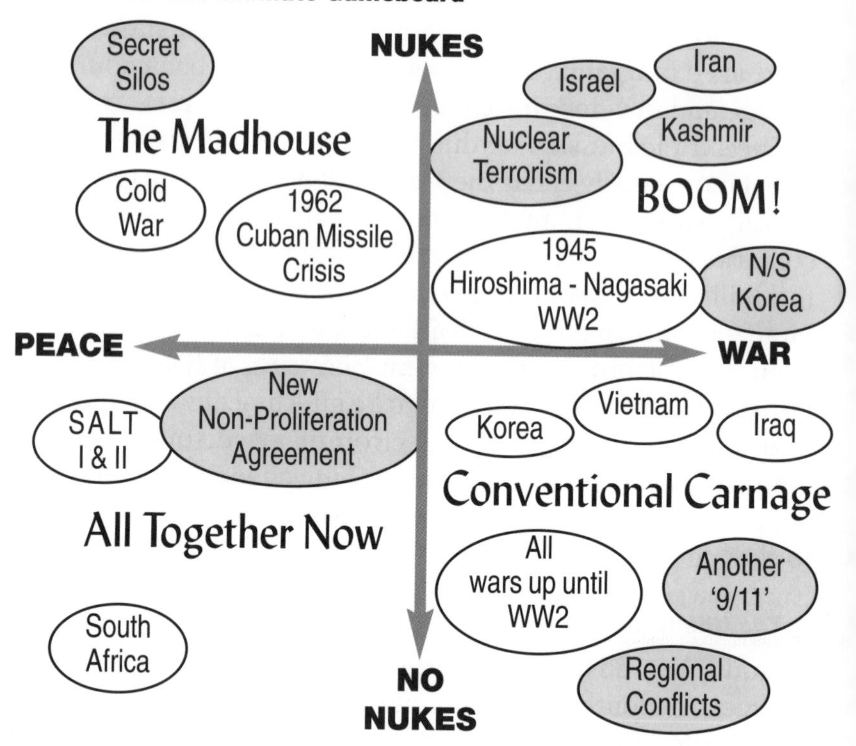

plotted past events (white ellipses) and possible future events (yellow ellipses).

Given, as we've mentioned, our proclivity for war, *Conventional Carnage* is a crowded spot and could see more regional conflicts or 9/11s. The *Madhouse* scenario is where the world has been since 1945 (briefly flirting with *Boom!* in 1962). The logic is that mutually assured destruction (MAD) will deter any nation from a first strike. Obviously, the advent of stateless terrorism has knocked this principle on the head since terrorists who plant nukes need have no fear of reprisals in a specific spot. They could be anywhere. Meanwhile, in this scenario, new nations build up secret silos to have at their disposal if attacked.

The *Boom!* zone has only been entered twice – on both occasions by America in Japan. As our yellow ellipses indicate, there are enough trouble spots around the world which can go nuclear and pose a real danger of another nuclear exchange. On top of which you must now add nuclear terrorism, where some shady member of the arms trade passes on a nuke for $25 million to a terrorist outfit. It could have been manufactured in a private laboratory in some secret location. And James Bond does not come to the rescue.

All Together Now is obviously the desired scenario where the world is at peace with no nukes. We put the Strategic Arms Limitation Talks between America and Russia in this quadrant, as well as South Africa that voluntarily dismantled its nuclear capability. But what is really needed is a new non-proliferation agreement that tackles the issue in a completely neutral manner. Hence the name of the scenario. For how can America or any country that currently has nukes take the moral high ground by arguing that other countries shouldn't have them? The only rationale they can offer is that they are more civilised and therefore more responsible than the have-nots. Such reasoning is definitely out of kilter with the modern notion of people of all colours and creeds being equal and therefore being treated equally. Maybe the West can single out some rogue states as too irresponsible to be trusted with nukes, but it begs the question of what constitutes a rogue state. Thus for any new agreement to be sustainable in the long run and have teeth, the 'haves' will have to come to the party and disgorge some of their nukes. All together now! Definitely not the form of headstrong hedgehogs.

However, John Nash – the mathematician in *A Beautiful Mind* – would approve of this scenario. In the movie, he is in a bar with friends when a blonde and several brunettes walk in. He advises that, instead of competing for the blonde (first prize for each of them), they should ask the brunettes out on the basis that this is the best outcome for the team. Otherwise, all but one of them are going to lose out as the brunettes, realising they are second choice, walk off in a huff. In real life, Nash won the Nobel Prize for his idea that games played in a co-operative fashion can lead to a higher level of equilibrium than pure rivalry. Nuclear games are no different, particularly as the West no longer has the supremacy to impose its own solution but equally has the most to lose.

Speakers' Corner

We'd like to end up our gameboard trio on a lighter note. Giving a speech in public has been recognised as one of the most stressful events anyone can ever face. The traditional advice of imagining the audience without their clothes on is only helpful for speakers who are avowed nudists. As speakers who prefer to keep our clothes on, we feel it is our duty to leave you with a gameboard that, hopefully, you will find particularly helpful when you are under the spotlight. It may be making a speech at a friend's wedding or presenting the annual report to anxious shareholders. Similarly, as someone who no doubt finds yourself at the receiving end of countless speeches and presentations, you can use this gameboard to score speakers. With content and delivery as the variables, the scenario gameboard – called *Speakers' Corner* – looks like the one opposite.

If the content of the speech is good but is lost in delivery (should one say translation?) it is *Buried Treasure*. If the content is shocking and it is delivered with all the panache of a wet blanket, it is *The Pits*. A blisteringly good delivery with memorable content peppered with anecdotal wit and real value earns the speaker an *Oscar*.

And the *Alpha Gamma*? There's an interesting story attached to this name. Many, many years ago one of us handed in a paper to a professor at Oxford. It was summarily returned with

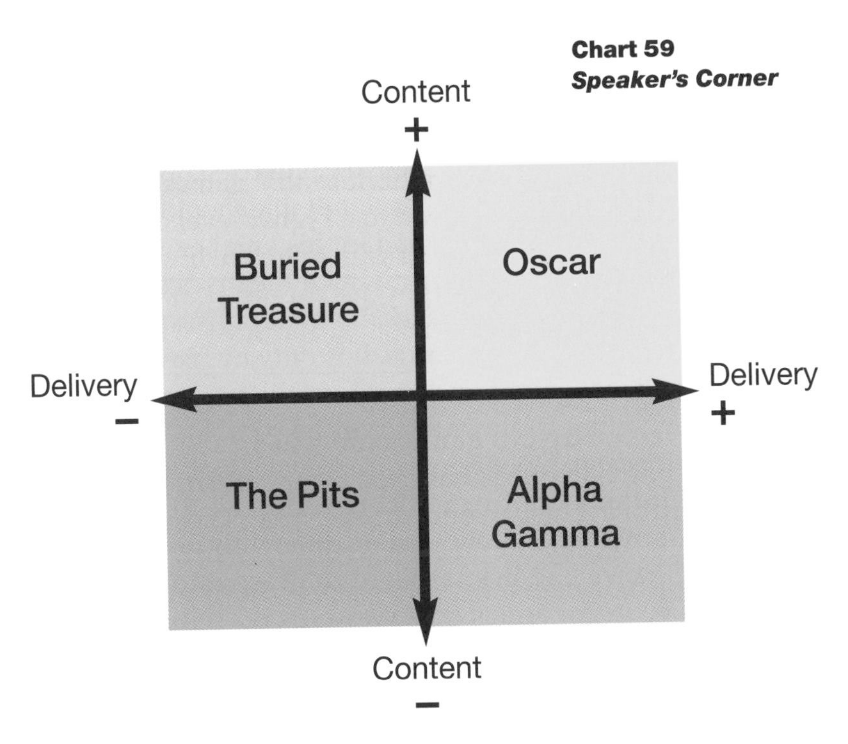

an alpha gamma grading. Not a top alpha, not an alpha minus, not even an alpha beta, but an alpha gamma. When challenged for an explanation, the professor simply replied the essay was "clever sh-t".

Here ends the lesson. You will have to judge for yourself the value and applicability of our conversation model. And the best way to do that is to test it in your own company. Do a reality check on your strategy; or evaluate your next project or takeover opportunity using our model.

Indeed, conversations are all the rage these days. Why do you think there has been such an enormous growth in personal executive coaches for CEOs? It's so they can have conversations on strategy and other things on a one-to-one basis. Not so much to learn new ideas from the coach, but to get their own ideas in order during the conversation. We just feel that it's equally important for executive teams to have these kinds of conversations so that they can get *their* thoughts in order too. Our model is designed to get the best out of everybody sitting around the table. And the table should be round, just like the one King Arthur had for his knights.

Above all, be a versatile fox, which means occasionally changing your mind when a *what if* materialises. Use your imagination and play scenarios. It is only by playing them that you will recognise a 'red flag' when it pops up. One organisation trying to stay ahead of the pack had to play a *Starving Greyhound* scenario to see how lack of cash might hinder its future performance. Better still, think of how the FBI and CIA might have followed up differently on leads, prior to 9/11, if we had been invited to present to them our scenario of a major attack on a Western city. It didn't come close to the actual deed, but the logic of the scenario, combined with a previously published warning on the serious challenge posed by fundamentalist Islam to Western lifestyle and values, might have opened their eyes to *possibilities* and *signs*. Fragments of the future contained in the present. It would certainly have sharpened their peripheral vision to the level of a fox.

Like Tilly Smith, the ten-year-old British girl who, because she had done a school project on tsunamis, recognised the abnormal withdrawal of the tide on Maikhao Beach in Phuket, Thailand for what it was – a 'red flag' for giant waves. According to Reuters, swift action by her mother and local hotel staff meant the beach was cleared before the tsunami arrived. It was one of the few beaches in Phuket where no one was killed.

So remember. Nobody is bigger than the game, especially when it involves Nature. And nothing, but nothing, can be discarded as a potential outcome. We live in extraordinary times. Let's talk about it and go on a strategic adventure.